THE BLADON LINES CHALET GIRLS' COOK BOOK

Roger Houghton
London

First published 1986

Edited and compiled by Sarah Litvinoff

Front, back cover and all text illustrations by Graham Thompson

Text © Bladon Lines Travel Ltd 1986

Illustrations © Roger Houghton Ltd 1986

All rights reserved. No part of this publication may be reproduced, stored in a retrieval system, or transmitted, in any form or by any means, electronic, mechanical, photocopying, recording or otherwise without the prior permission of Roger Houghton Ltd

Set in Garamond by Gee Graphics Ltd

Printed and bound in Great Britain by Biddles Ltd, Guildford for Roger Houghton Ltd, in association with J.M. Dent and Sons Ltd, Aldine House, 33 Welbeck Street, London W1M 8LX

British Library Cataloguing in Publication Data
The Bladon Lines chalet girls' cook book.
  1. Dinners and dining
  I. Bladon Lines
  641.5'68   TX737

ISBN 1 85203 001 1

Contents

Foreword by Mark Lines	7
Starters	11
Main Courses	47
Beef – Veal – Chicken and Turkey – Lamb – Pork – Fish – Pasta	
Vegetables and Salads	89
Puddings	105
Cakes	137
Drinks	149
Index	155

FOREWORD

By Mark Lines, co-founder of Bladon Lines

Bladon Lines Travel is the country's biggest operator of staffed chalet parties in ski resorts. Each winter season we employ around two hundred girls, aged between twenty and twenty-five, who go out to the Alps and have to cook for our customers from mid-December to the end of April. Each day, for these four and a half months, the girls provide their guests with a cooked breakfast, a picnic lunch, tea and dinner. The style of the menus that the girls cook was, in the early days of chalet party holidays, always loosely described as Cordon Bleu and indeed many of the girls have attended that excellent school. Over the years, however, the limitations of chalet cooking and the ingenuity of young cooks working under pressure have produced some interesting and original recipes and it is these that we present in this book.

This book is *not* intended to be an instructional manual for the would-be chalet girl. It is a compilation of some of the best recipes and practical tips of our old hands. It will be a valuable part of the kitchen library of all young or thrifty cooks since it will teach you how to impress your friends in a cramped flat and how to give a big dinner party for a reasonable price.

More than this, they are recipes that, for the most part, can be produced rapidly. Any chalet girl worth her salt will be a keen skier and she'll want to spend the maximum number of hours out of the chalet and on the mountainside. We don't let our girls cut corners, but they do become experts at knocking up a stunning meal in a couple of hours. This is an invaluable skill for any working cook.

If you *are* a prospective Chalet Girl, don't be discouraged! Take this book to the slopes with you – it will prove invaluable. If you are a busy, creative cook, try the recipes at home; we are sure you'll find them as easy to use and that the results will be just as good at sea level as they are at 6000 feet.

Note on the recipes

All these recipes are devised by chalet girls past and present who have cooked them – sometimes under difficult conditions – for their guests. None of them have been copied from other books; most of them have been handed down from friends, mothers, grandmothers, other chalet girls – or simply made up. Some of the most triumphant started out as disasters or as improvisations with ingredients that just came to hand, and have been added to the girl's repertoire because they turned out to be such a success.

The estimates as to how many each recipe feeds have been suggested by the chalet girls. Some of them have big appetites, and are used to feeding groups who similarly eat a lot; others are more dainty eaters. The amounts *will* feed the number suggested, but how heftily will vary a little from recipe to recipe.

STARTERS

'In some ways the most important course at dinner is the first course. Something unusual puts the guests in the right mood. Even if it is not grand, a garnish or trimming gives it a sense of occasion. To supply Melba toast with egg mousse, or to serve soup with a herb loaf or garlic bread, or croûtons makes a lot of difference for hardly any extra cost.' *The Bladon Lines Chalet Girl Manual*

TUNA FISH CREAMS

225 g (8 oz) tin of tuna fish
5 hard-boiled eggs, chopped
2 or 3 tomatoes, peeled and
　chopped
30 ml (2 tablespoons) capers
90 ml (6 tablespoons) single cream

300 ml (½ pint) mayonnaise
juice of 1 lemon
15 ml (1 tablespoon) powdered
　gelatine
45 ml (3 tablespoons) water

(serves 10–12)

Mix together the cream, mayonnaise, and lemon juice, and season to taste. Mix the gelatine with water, heat over a pan of simmering water until the gelatine dissolves. Allow to cool, and then add it to the cream mixture with the remaining ingredients. Pile into ramekins and leave to set. Garnish with thin slices of cucumber and tomato.

SMOKED MACKEREL PATE

225 g (8 oz) smoked mackerel
　(canned or fresh), skinned
125 g (4 oz) butter
30 ml (2 tablespoons) double
　cream
(serves 6–8)

30 ml (2 tablesponns)
mayonnaise
juice of 1 lemon
4 drops tabasco

Put all ingredients in a food processor and blend well. Serve chilled with hot French bread.

TUNA FISH AND SPINACH TERRINE

2 x 225 g (8 oz) boxes frozen chopped spinach
50 g (2 oz) melted butter or margarine
225 g (8 oz) tin tuna fish
225 g (8 oz) fromage blanc
150 ml (¼ pint) double cream

juice of 1 lemon
nutmeg
15 ml (1 tablespoon) powdered gelatine
60 ml (4 tablespoons) water
salt and pepper

(serves 10–12)

Cook spinach according to the instructions and drain well. Mix with the butter or margarine and season with salt, pepper and nutmeg. Allow to cool. Dissolve gelatine in the water. Add half this mixture to the cooked spinach. Put the tuna, fromage blanc, cream and lemon juice in the food processor and blend (or mash together). Turn into a bowl, add seasoning to taste, and add the rest of the gelatine mixture. Mix well. Oil a loaf tin approximately 22.5 cm x 8 cm (9 in x 3½ in). Spread half the spinach mixture on the bottom, followed by half the tuna mixture. Repeat the layers. Chill until it is time to serve. Dip the tin in hot water to loosen the terrine. Cut into slices and put on individual plates, garnishing with a twist of lemon.

Chalet girl comment: You can make this the night before – or in the morning.

ST ANTON SARDINE PATE

450 g (1 lb) box of frozen spinach, defrosted and drained
2 tins of sardines (in tomato sauce)

juice of ½ lemon
salt and pepper

(serves 6)

Put spinach into the food processor, add the sardines (with the backbones removed) and juice, and blend until really smooth. Turn out into a bowl, add more lemon juice and seasoning to taste. Serve slightly chilled, with a slice of lemon for garnish.

Chalet girl comment: It doesn't look beautiful, but after tasting it the guests really love it and want the recipe!

TUNA MOUSSE

225 g (8 oz) tin tuna fish
12 g (½ oz) powdered gelatine
500 g (1 lb) Ricotta cheese (or cream cheese, or cottage cheese)
45 ml (3 tablespoons) natural yoghurt
1 chicken stock cube
10 ml (2 teaspoons) fresh dill, or fresh chopped parsley

(serves 6)

Dissolve the chicken stock cube with a little boiling water and add the gelatine. Put tuna fish, cheese and yoghurt in the food processor and blend well. Fold in the gelatine mixture and the chopped dill or parsley. Pile the mixture into a nice dish and place in the fridge to set. Serve with warm brown bread.

Chalet girl comment: Everyone enjoys it!

DOUBLE-QUICK PATE

3 x 200 g (7 oz) tins tuna fish
30 ml (2 tablespoons) mayonnaise
125 g (4 oz) butter
30 ml (2 tablespoons) cream or yoghurt
salt and pepper

(serves 6)

Mash together all the ingredients, season to taste and chill. Serve with thin slices of toast.

BL Chalet Girl economy tip
Check out your local shops and supermarkets so that you know where to find the cheapest ingredients, and make a regular note of prices. Plan all your menus for the week. Write down all the ingredients you are going to need for each day, and how much you need of each commodity for the week. Then estimate what your weekly shop should cost. If it is more than you can afford, you can replan your menus now, before it is too late!

PRAWNS AND SPINACH EN COCOTTE

450 g (1 lb) tin of puréed spinach (or frozen equivalent)
2 x 175 g (6 oz) tins of prawns (or frozen equivalent)
125–150 g (4–5 oz) carton of fromage blanc
(serves 6)

juice of 1 lemon
25 g (1 oz) grated cheese
75 g (3 oz) breadcrumbs
salt and pepper

Divide the spinach between 6 ramekin dishes. If using frozen spinach, defrost, drain, and season very well. Drain prawns and place evenly on top of spinach. Add the lemon juice to the fromage blanc, season well, and cover prawns with this mixture. Mix the grated cheese and breadcrumbs, and sprinkle over the top. Place under the grill until brown and bubbling. Serve with hot, herb bread (see p.45).

Chalet girl comment: Prawns can be replaced by hard-boiled eggs, crab-meat, or left-over, cooked white fish.

SALAMI EN COCOTTE

8 eggs
croûtons made from 8 slices of bread, trimmed, diced and fried in oil
(serves 8)

8 oz salami, diced
120 ml (8 tablespoons) thick cream
salt and pepper

Place the croûtons in the bottom of 8 ramekins. Cover with a layer of salami. Crack an egg over this, then sprinkle with salt and pepper and cover with 15 ml (1 tablespoon) of cream per ramekin. Place in a roasting dish, and pour water round the ramekins, to come half-way up the sides. Cover with another baking dish and bake in a moderate oven (350°F, 180°C, gas 4) for 6–8 minutes. Sprinkle with parsley and serve at once.

Each resort has an MBO, a handyman who, because of the nature of his duties, is usually a big lad. There is dispute about whether the initials stand for Muscle Bound Oaf or Maintenance and Buildings Officer. One such beefy but benign character in Courmayeur was slumbering peacefully in his bed on the top floor of a chalet, on a quiet frosty night after a busy day maintaining and building. What he didn't know was that an amorous customer was on the lookout for one of the chalet girls to whom he had taken a strong fancy. This guest had already taken quite a bit of liquid refreshment and consequently decided that tonight was the night.

Believing that a softly-softly approach was the best policy, the guest felt his way, without putting the lights on, to what he thought was the right door. Tiptoeing quietly across the floor, he threw back the covers and fell with wild cries upon what he believed to be his quarry, and was in fact the brawny MBO. Rumour has it that neither has been the same since.

CARY'S COURMAYEUR COCOTTE

8 medium tomatoes, peeled
8 rashers streaky bacon (crisply cooked)
3 avocados, peeled and stoned
125g (4 oz) Stilton

300 ml (½ pint) vinaigrette dressing (see p.104)
2 loaves hot herb bread (see p.45)

(serves 8)

Dice the tomatoes and the avocado flesh. Crumble the Stilton, and slice the bacon into small pieces. Mix all together in a large bowl with the French dressing. Divide into ramekins and serve with hot herb bread.

EGGS IN CONSOMME

8 eggs
1 tube 'Le Parfait' pâté or home-made chicken-liver pâté

2 x 275 g (10 oz) tins condensed beef consommé

(serves 8)

Boil eggs for 5 minutes. Plunge into cold water and peel *carefully* – it is easy to break the white. Squeeze a twirl of pâté into the bottom of each ramekin. When eggs are quite cold, place one in each ramekin. Pour over liquid consommé. Leave in fridge to set for at least 3 hours. Serve with hot French bread.

Chalet girl comment: An easy dish to do in advance.

SALMON RAMEKINS

2 x 225 g (8 oz) tins salmon
150 ml (¼ pint) single cream
1 finely chopped onion
75 g (3 oz) flour
125 g (4 oz) butter

4 hard-boiled eggs
450 ml (¾ pint) milk
125 g (4 oz) cheese
50 g (2 oz) breadcrumbs
salt and pepper

(serves 10-12)

Fry the onion in 75 g (3 oz) butter until soft. Stir in the flour, and then make a white sauce with the milk. Cook until thick. Season to taste, and then add the cream. Mix in the roughly chopped eggs, and add the drained, flaked – and boned – salmon. Divide the mixture between 10 ramekins. Sprinkle with cheese. Fry the breadcrumbs in the rest of the butter and sprinkle over the cheese. Place in a pre-heated moderate oven (350°F, 180°C, gas 4) for 15 minutes, until heated through.

BACON CREAM

8 rashers bacon, de-rinded
2 beaten eggs
225 g (8 oz) grated Cheddar
300 ml (½ pint) whipping cream

150 ml (¼ pint) milk
cayenne pepper
salt and pepper

(serves 8)

Fry bacon until crisp, chop and divide it between 8 ramekins. Grate the cheese and put half of it on top of the bacon. Mix remaining cheese, eggs, cream, milk and seasoning together, and divide between the ramekins. Put the ramekins in a baking tin and fill with water to come half-way up the sides. Bake in a moderate oven (325°–350°F, 170°–180°C, gas 3–4) for 25–30 minutes until set. They should be wobbly (but not too liquid).

BL Chalet Girl economy tip
Grate your ration of cooking cheese once a week and keep it covered in a bowl in the fridge. It saves time and makes it go further too.

SPINACH RAMEKIN

2 x 225 g (8 oz) frozen chopped spinach
2 large eggs, beaten

125 g (4 oz) grated cheese
pinch of grated nutmeg
150 ml (¼ pint) single cream

(serves 8)

Cook the frozen spinach as directed. Drain and let it cool slightly, then add all the other ingredients and mix well. Divide mixture into 8 ramekins and bake in pre-heated moderate oven (350°F, 180°C, gas 4) for about 15 minutes.

CRANS MONTANA RAMEKINS

12 eggs
12 rashers of bacon
10 ml (2 teaspoons) Worcester sauce
50 g (2 oz) butter

50 g (2 oz) flour
600 ml (1 pint) milk
125 g (4 oz) grated cheese
50 g (2 oz) breadcrumbs

(serves 8)

Hard-boil eggs and roughly chop them. Fry bacon until crisp and chop into small pieces. Melt the butter and stir in the flour. Cook for 1–2 minutes, and then gradually blend in the milk, stirring all the time. Cook for 5 minutes. Add the Worcester sauce and cheese and mix in the bacon and eggs. Divide between 8 ramekins. Cover the top with breadcrumbs and put into a pre-heated, moderately hot oven (400°F, 200°C, gas 6) for 15 minutes before serving.

Chalet girl comment: This is very quick, easy and cheap – but extremely tasty. For a more expensive dish you can use prawns instead of bacon.

A travel agent's convention arrived at one of the resorts, and one of the party asked about the Bladon Lines staff. He was told that they were divided into reps, chalet girls and 'Mother Superiors'. The latter to look after the chalet girls and the chalets.

One of the Mother Superiors was assigned to the party to show them around. On the way home, the travel agent said regretfully to the Bladon Lines sales manager, 'Pity about that girl being a nun – I really fancied her.'

OEUF EN COCOTTE

8 eggs
225 g (8 oz) shelled prawns
300 ml (½ pint) milk
12 g (½ oz) butter
12 g (½ oz) flour
60 ml (4 tablespoons) dry white wine

60 ml (4 tablespoons) double cream
50 g (2 oz) Gruyère cheese, grated

(serves 8)

Melt the butter and stir in the flour. Cook gently for 1–2 minutes, and then gradually add the milk, stirring all the time. Cook for 5 minutes. Add the white wine and prawns. Divide this mixture between 8 ramekin dishes. Break an egg on top of each, and divide the cream between them. Sprinkle with grated cheese. Place in a pre-heated, very hot oven (475°F, 250°C, gas 9) for 4 minutes.
Then place under the grill until the top is brown and bubbling. Serve with fresh French bread.

Chalet girl comment: This is very quick to make and absolutely everyone raves about it.

POIRE ROQUEFORT

4 ripe pears, peeled and diced
4 slices of white bread
oil for frying
225 g (8 oz) blue cheese,
(Roquefort or Danish Blue), thinly sliced
120 ml (8 tablespoons) cream

(serves 8)

Cut bread into 1 cm (½ in cubes) and fry in hot oil until golden brown. Place the croûtons in 8 ovenproof ramekins. Place pieces of pear on top of the croûtons. Divide the blue cheese between the ramekins. Dribble one tablespoon of cream on top of each ramekin. Grill for 10 minutes until golden brown.

FLEMISH EGGS

8 hard-boiled eggs, sliced
12 g (½ oz) butter
12 g (½ oz) flour
300 ml (½ pint) milk
2 cloves of garlic, crushed
10 ml (2 teaspoons) chopped parsley
125 g (4 oz) grated cheese
60 ml (4 tablespoons) double cream
salt and pepper

(serves 8)

Divide the eggs between 8 ramekins. Melt the butter and stir in the flour. Cook gently for 1–2 minutes, and then gradually add the milk, stirring all the time. Cook for 5 minutes. Add garlic, parsley, cream – and seasoning to taste. Pour the sauce over the eggs, and top with grated cheese. Grill for 6–8 minutes or until golden brown.

BL Chalet Girl kitchen planner tip
Keep a large jar for strained cooking oil from deep-frying or roasting.

HADDOCK SURPRISE

450 g (1 lb) smoked haddock, fresh or frozen
125 (4 oz) prawns
4 slices of ham
600 ml (1 pint) milk
50 g (2 oz) butter
50 g (2 oz) flour
175 g (6 oz) Cheddar cheese, grated
75 g (3 oz) breadcrumbs
salt and pepper

(serves 8)

Poach the haddock in the milk. Strain, and reserve milk. Skin and divide the haddock among 8 ramekins. Chop the ham, and place on top of the haddock. Do the same with the prawns. Melt the butter, mix in the flour and cook for 1–2 minutes. Gradually add the reserved milk, stirring all the time, and cook for 5 minutes. Mix in half the grated cheese. Season to taste. Pour over the mixture in the ramekins. Mix the remaining cheese with the breadcrumbs, and sprinkle over the sauce. Put in a pre-heated, hot oven (425°–475°F, 220°–250°C, gas 7–9) for 10 minutes, then take out and grill until the top is brown and bubbling. Serve immediately.

WINTERSONNE SOUP

3 large onions, peeled
8 rashers of bacon, de-rinded
175 g (6 oz) tin of red peppers, drained
800 g (1¾ lb) tin of tomatoes
1.2 litres (2 pints) good chicken stock
300 ml (½ pint) single cream or yoghurt
salt and pepper

(serves 8)

Chop onions and bacon and fry together, adding a little oil if necessary. Chop the red peppers and add to the bacon and onions. Then add the tomatoes with their juice and stock. Taste, season and simmer. Liquidise in the blender. Serve with cream or yoghurt swirled through.

GRENOUILLES

500g (1lb 2oz) frozen frogs' legs, thawed
2 medium onions
2 cloves garlic
30 ml (2 tablespoons) double cream

50 g (2 oz) butter
15 ml (1 tablespoon) fresh, finely chopped parsley
5 ml (1 teaspoon) dried tarragon
300–450 ml (½–¾ pint) wine
salt and pepper

(serves 8)

Finely chop the onions, crush the garlic and sauté gently in the butter until soft. Add the frogs' legs and wine, cover pan, and simmer very gently for 10–15 minutes. Add cream, season, and add the parsley and tarragon. Serve with fresh French bread.

SOUPE DE POISSON

450 g (1 lb) cooked white fish
225 g (8 oz) tin cooked mussels
2 litres (5 pints) fish stock
125 g (4 oz) butter
1 clove garlic, crushed
225 g (8 oz) unshelled prawns

accompaniments
4 slices white bread
125 g (4 oz) grated cheese
oil for frying
salt and pepper
15 ml (1 tablespoon) tomato purée

750 g (1¾ lb) tin tomatoes, liquidised
15 ml (1 tablespoon) tomato purée
125 g (4 oz) plain flour

1 clove garlic, crushed
300 ml (½ pint) mayonnaise (preferably home-made)

(serves 8–10)

Skin and flake the white fish and set to one side. Shell the prawns. Reserve the flesh and fry the shells in the butter till the butter turns brown. Strain the shells, keeping the butter. To the butter, add the flour and cook for 1 minute. Mix in the tomato purée and the garlic, and cook for a further minute. Slowly pour in the fish stock a little at a time, stirring constantly. Now add the tomatoes, taste, and season.

Simmer for 20 minutes and stir in the fish, prawns and mussels.

Accompaniments
Mix mayonnaise with tomato purée and crushed garlic, and serve in individual ramekins. Cut bread into large squares, measuring approximately 4 cm (1½ in), and fry until golden. Hand the grated cheese separately.

One chalet hotel has a zippy little dumb waiter, connecting kitchen to dining room. At dinner one night, it zoomed up carrying twenty-two chocolate mousses, hiccupped uncontrollably at the top — and shot the mousses over the expectant diners.

THIRTEEN STAR SALAD

1 large carton of natural yoghurt
150 g (5 oz) blue cheese (Roquefort, Cambozola or Danish Blue)

8 heads of chicory
8 oranges
8 apples
125 g (4 oz) sultanas
salt and pepper

(serves 8)

Mix the yoghurt and cheese together, and season. Slice the chicory; peel and slice the oranges; core and slice the apples. Then mix the chicory, fruit and sultanas with the yoghurt dressing. Serve garnished with twists of orange, accompanied by herb bread (see p.45).

MARINATED MUSHROOMS

1 kg (2½ lbs) mushrooms, preferably very small
½ litre (15 fl oz) vinaigrette dressing (see p.104)
4 cloves crushed garlic

½ litre (15 fl oz) dry white wine
30 ml (2 tablespoons) fresh chives or 15 ml (1 tablespoon) dried

(serves 8)

Wash the mushrooms thoroughly, trimming stalks if necessary. Blend the wine, crushed garlic and chives with the vinaigrette dressing. Pour this over the mushrooms and mix well. Leave to marinate overnight, or all day. Serve in ramekins garnished with parsley and lots of fresh bread to soak up the dressing.

AVOCADO PATE AUX QUATRE SAISONS

4 avocados, peeled and stoned
150 ml (¼ pint) mayonnaise (preferably home-made)
juice of 2 lemons
1 sachet Davis's powdered gelatine

2 small cloves garlic
350 ml (12 fl oz) dry white wine
150 ml (¼ pint) whipping cream
4 egg whites, stiffly beaten

(serves 8)

Dissolve the gelatine in 3 tablespoons of the wine in a small bowl over hot water. Blend the avocados with the remaining white wine and lemon juice. Add gelatine, crushed garlic and mayonnaise. Half whip the cream and fold into the mixture with the whisked egg whites. Pour into ramekins, and put into the fridge to set. Serve with thinly sliced brown bread.

STUFFED GRAPEFRUIT

4 large grapefruit
1 225 g (8 oz) tub cottage cheese
1 125 g (4 oz) packet herb cheese
1 green pepper, de-seeded
1 green apple, cored
1 cucumber

5 ml (1 teaspoon) mixed Herbes de Provence
Worcester sauce
salt and pepper
parsley sprigs

(serves 8)

Cut the grapefruit in half and scoop the segments into a bowl, removing skin and pith. Chop the apple, pepper and cucumber into 1 cm (¼ in) cubes. Keep back some cucumber to slice for garnish. Add the cubes to the grapefruit flesh, mix in cheeses, herbs – and the Worcester sauce and seasoning to taste. Pile into the grapefruit halves, and garnish with parsley and twists of cucumber slices.

BL Chalet Girl garnish
A spoonful of yoghurt, soured cream or double cream in each bowl of soup looks nice and tastes good.

PARSNIP SOUP

75 g (3 oz) butter or margarine
1 large parsnip
125 g (4 oz) chopped onion
1 clove garlic
15 ml (1 tablespoon) flour
2 large potatoes

5 ml (1 teaspoon) curry powder
1 litre (2 pints) good stock
150 ml (¼ pint) single cream
chives to decorate
salt and pepper

(serves 6)

Peel and slice the parsnip. Peel and dice the potatoes. Gently cook the onion, parsnip and potatoes in the butter until the onion is soft. Add crushed garlic, curry powder and flour, and mix well. Slowly blend in the stock. Cover, and simmer till cooked. Liquidise in the blender. Taste, season, and reheat. Just before serving, add the cream and garnish with chives. Serve with croûtons (see p.46).

GORGONZOLA MOUSSE

125 g (4 oz) Gorgonzola *
2 egg yolks
3 egg whites
25 g (1 oz) powdered gelatine
30 ml (2 tablespoons) water

150 ml (¼ pint) natural yoghurt
tabasco
parsley
salt and pepper

(serves 6)

Dissolve the gelatine in the water in a small bowl over hot water. Beat the egg yolks with 30 ml (2 tablespoons) of the yoghurt. Add the gelatine. Mash the cheese with the rest of the yoghurt (or blend in food processor) and add the egg-yolk mixture. Season with salt, pepper and tabasco. Meanwhile, beat the egg whites until stiff, and then fold into the cheese mixture. Pour this mixture into individual ramekins and leave for at least 4 hours. Sprinkle with finely chopped parsley before serving.

Chalet girl comment: Very rich – but yumbos!

* *The more gooey the better!*

One day the St Anton rep was escorting a coach full of customers from the resort back to the airport at the end of their holiday. At the border with Switzerland the bus was stopped by the customs men and thoroughly searched. They pulled out the baggage and inspected it carefully – and then brought in the sniffer dogs. As the rep anxiously checked his watch, fearing that the customers would miss the plane, the dogs homed in on an offending suitcase.

The case and its terrified owner were whisked off to a little room. The case was opened and there inside was . . . a chicken sandwich.

MONKEY'S DELIGHT

1 banana per person
1 slice of ham per banana
600 ml (1 pint) of good cheese sauce per 4 bananas
25 g (1 oz) grated cheese per 4 bananas

Peel the bananas and roll each one in a slice of ham. Place in roasting tin, and pour the cheese sauce over the top. Sprinkle with grated cheese and bake in a pre-heated, moderate oven (350°F, 180°C, gas 4) for 20–30 minutes, until cooked through. If the top is not brown enough, flash under the grill for a minute or two.

Chalet girl comment: Sounds unlikely, but is really delicious.

CROISSANTS A LA MAISON ROSE

6 croissants
6 slices ham
125 g (4 oz) mushrooms
300 ml (½ pint) béchamel sauce
75 g (3oz) grated Cheddar cheese
1 onion, chopped

12 g (½ oz) butter
Dijon mustard
30 ml (2 tablespoons) chopped parsley
salt and pepper

(serves 6)

Sweat the chopped onion in the butter, slice the mushrooms and add them to the onions. Cook gently until soft. Meanwhile, slice the croissants in half, spread with a little mustard, then place the slices of ham on the bottom halves. Cover the ham with grated cheese. Place the croissant bottoms uncovered in a pre-heated, hot oven (450°F, 230°C, gas 8) for 10–15 minutes, or until the cheese has melted. Put the top halves in the oven as well. Check that the croissants don't burn. Mix the mushrooms, onions and chopped parsley into the béchamel. Taste, and season. When the croissants are ready, put the lower halves on individual plates, divide the sauce between them, and pop the top back on. Garnish with lettuce and tomato.

PASTA A L'INDIENNE

1 500 g (1 lb 2 oz) packet of pasta shells
15 ml (1 tablespoon) oil
4 large spicy sausages
1 300 g (11 oz) packet sultanas
450 g (1 lb) peanuts
600 ml (1 pint) mayonnaise

60–90 ml (4–6 teaspoons) Madras curry paste
1 lettuce
30 ml (2 tablespoons) browned, flaked almonds
salt and pepper

(serves 10–14)

Cook the pasta shells in plenty of water with the 15 ml (1 tablespoon) of oil, and then drain. Cut the sausages into small cubes and fry them. Mix the curry paste into the mayonnaise, and season to taste. Add the peanuts, sultanas, sausage cubes and pasta, and mix well together. Serve in individual plates on top of a lettuce leaf, and sprinkle with the flaked almonds.

MUSHROOMS A LA LAMASTRA

25 g (1 oz) butter or margarine
1 medium onion, finely diced
150 g (6 oz) mushrooms
25 g (1 oz) plain flour
15 ml (1 tablespoon) parsley

300 ml (½ pint) milk
2 tomatoes
125 g (4 oz) breadcrumbs
25 g (1 oz) grated cheese

(serves 6)

Gently cook the onion in the butter or margarine until soft. Add the mushrooms, finely chopped, and fry until cooked. Take the saucepan from the heat and add the flour, stirring well. Then add the milk gradually, and bring to the boil. Taste and season, and add the chopped parsley. Divide this mixture between 6 ramekins. Peel the tomatoes (by cutting a small cross in the skin, and soaking them in boiling water for 30 seconds), slice them into 3 pieces each, and place on top of the mushroom sauce in the ramekins. Mix the grated cheese with the breadcrumbs, and sprinkle this over the tomato slices. Put the ramekins on a baking sheet, and put in a pre-heated moderate oven (400°F, 200°C, gas 6) for about 10 minutes, until the mixture has thoroughly heated and the breadcrumbs have browned. Serve with either herb or garlic bread (see pp. 45 and 46).

BL Chalet Girl garnish
If you have a heart-shaped cutter you could make your croûtons more romantic by cutting the bread with it.

DEEP-FRIED MUSHROOMS WITH HERB CHEESE

450 g (1 lb) button mushrooms
225 g (8 oz) herb cheese, grated

125 g (4 oz) plain flour, seasoned
125 g (4 oz) white breadcrumbs
4 beaten eggs

(serves 8)

Wash and remove the stalks from the mushrooms. Fill each one with herb cheese. Roll each mushroom in the flour, then the beaten egg, and then the breadcrumbs. Make sure that the mushrooms and filling are completely covered in the egg and breadcrumbs, as the cheese tends to leak when cooked. Deep fry until brown. Serve the mushrooms on small side plates, garnished with a wedge of tomato and a sprig of parsley.

AVOCADO MARSEILLES

3 avocados
2 green peppers
2 red peppers
½ small cucumber

garnish
lemon slices
tomato quarters

(serves 6)

300 ml (½ pint) mayonnaise
1 clove garlic, crushed
½ iceberg lettuce

cucumber slices
sprigs of parsley

Peel and stone the avocados and dice them. Remove seeds from the cucumber and peppers, and dice. Thin down the mayonnaise with a little milk, and mix in the crushed garlic. Fold in the avocados, cucumber and pepper dice. Thinly slice the iceberg lettuce and use to line individual dishes. Pile the avocado mixture on top. Garnish each portion with a twisted slice of lemon, a slice of cucumber, a quarter of tomato and a sprig of parsley.

Chalet girl comment: As individual dishes these look extremely presentable, and only take about 10 minutes. It is an excellent way to use up avocados that will get too soft if left another day.

One of the best, cosiest chalets in Verbier is built in the traditional wooden style, and the walls are decorated with the stuffed heads of some of the local wildlife – chamois and the like. A particularly jokey group of guests decided to play a trick on their chalet girl and popped one of these heads into the chalet's oven before going to bed one night.

Next morning the girl came down to cook breakfast, turned on the oven to pre-heat it, and got on with her chores. It was a little while before she noticed a peculiar smell, and a little bit longer before she opened the oven door and got the shock of her life!

BAKED AVOCADO

4 avocados
175 g (6 oz) tin of tuna fish
225 g (8 oz) mushrooms
75 g (3 oz) butter

50 g (2 oz) flour
600 ml (1 pint) milk
125 g (4 oz) Cheddar cheese, grated

(serves 8)

Cook the sliced mushrooms in 25 g (1 oz) butter until tender. Drain the tuna fish and flake it. Cut the avocados in half, stone, and scoop out the flesh and chop it coarsely, saving the skins. Melt the rest of the butter, stir in the flour and cook for 1–2 minutes. Blend in the milk and cook for 8 minutes, stirring occasionally. Add the grated cheese. Put the cheese sauce in a bowl and fold in the avocado, mushrooms and tuna. Fill the avocado skins with this mixture and bake in a pre-heated, moderate oven (350°F, 180°C, gas 4) for 30 minutes.

GSTAAD MUSHROOMS

1 kg (2½ lbs) mushrooms
35 g (1½ oz) butter
3 medium onions, peeled
3 cloves garlic
½ bottle red wine
50 g (2 oz) tin tomato purée
6 rashers of bacon, de-rinded
4 oz walnuts

5 ml (1 teaspoon) Worcester sauce
tabasco
5 ml (1 teaspoon) mixed herbs
1 bay leaf
pinch of nutmeg
5 ml (1 teaspoon) sugar
salt and pepper

(serves 8)

Chop onions and garlic and fry in the butter until transparent. Clean and trim mushrooms and add them whole to the pan with the herbs, nutmeg, sugar, Worcester sauce and seasoning to taste. Add drops of tabasco to taste. Pour in the wine and reduce to ¼ the amount. Stir in the tomato purée. Take out bay leaf. Grill the bacon till crisp, chop and add to the pan. Finally, chop the walnuts roughly and add them to the mixture. Serve in small, individual dishes with melba toast or fresh bread.

Chalet girl comment: An interesting starter – very good for using up dregs of wine.

> *BL Chalet Girl economy tip*
> Left-over vegetables are ideal for soups. Liquidise them quickly and add cream or milk and plenty of spices. Serve hot or cold.

DEVILLED MUSHROOMS

450 g (1 lb) button mushrooms
50 g (2 oz) butter
300 ml (½ pint) cream
30 ml (2 tablespoons) tomato ketchup
10 ml (2 teaspoons) Worcester sauce
5 ml (1 teaspoon) mustard
10 ml (2 teaspoons) wine vinegar
pinch of nutmeg
75 g (3 oz) grated cheese

(serves 8)

Fry the mushrooms whole in the butter. Place in ovenproof dish **and then add** all the other ingredients except the cheese. Cover with grated cheese and bake for 10 minutes in a pre-heated, moderately hot oven (400°F, 200°C, gas 6).

CHAMPIGNONS A LA CREME

450 g (1 lb) mushrooms *
125 g (4 oz) butter
1 clove garlic, crushed
90 ml (6 tablespoons) double cream
parsley
salt and pepper

(serves 6)

Clean and trim the mushrooms and put in an ovenproof dish. Melt the butter and mix in the garlic and some seasoning. Pour the mixture over the mushrooms evenly. Cover with the cream and bake in a moderate oven (350°F, 180°C, gas 4) for about 25 minutes. Sprinkle with chopped parsley and serve immediately.

Chalet girl comment: This is delicious and really easy.

* The large, flat ones are best.

MUSHROOM STROGANOFF

1 large onion, sliced
4 sticks of celery, sliced
450 g (1 lb) button mushrooms, sliced
50 g (2 oz) butter
50 g (2 oz) flour
300 ml (½ pint) water or chicken stock

pinch of thyme
pinch of ground bay leaves
300 ml (½ pint) soured cream
fresh, chopped parsley
salt and pepper

(serves 6)

Sauté the onions and celery in the butter. Stir in the flour, add the water or stock, herbs and cream. Add the mushrooms, cook for a few minutes, taste and adjust seasoning. Sprinkle with chopped parsley before serving.

SEAFOOD ENVELOPES

225 g (8 oz) cooked prawns
225 g (8 oz) cooked mussels
sprig of parsley
5 ml (1 teaspoon) tomato purée
50 g (2 oz) butter
2 bay leaves
2 beaten eggs
salt and pepper
225 g (8 oz) white fish fillet
600 ml (1 pint) milk

30 ml (2 tablespoons) lemon juice
6 peppercorns
60 g (2 oz) flour
450 g (1 lb) frozen puff pastry
oil for deep frying
king prawns for garnish (optional)
1 lemon, sliced
fresh, chopped parsley

(serves 8)

If frozen, defrost the prawns slowly, then sprinkle with black pepper and lemon juice. Place the white fish in a pan, cover with milk, and add the peppercorns, bay leaves, and parsley sprig. Season with salt. Place over a gentle heat and simmer slowly for 4 minutes. Cool, skin, then flake, reserving the milk.

Melt the butter in a small pan, add the flour, and cook for 30 seconds. Remove from heat and add the strained milk from the fish into the pan, stirring well. Return pan to the heat, and bring slowly to the boil, stirring continuously. Season, and add tomato purée. Simmer for 1 minute.

Stir in the fish, prawns and mussels, and allow to cool.

Defrost the pastry and roll it out into thin squares 12 cm x 12 cm (5 in x 5 in). Put one tablespoon of the fish mixture on each square (saving half the mixture for decoration). Fold the squares in half diagonally, sticking the edges well together with beaten egg. Brush both sides of the pastry with more beaten egg. Deep fry, a few at a time, until golden brown. Drain well on kitchen paper. Serve at once, decorated with the rest of the sauce, slices of lemon and parsley. For extra panache, you can top each envelope with one king prawn.

Another Bladon Lines way of coping with a culinary disaster is to get the customers to see the funny side of it. One girl made a delicious terrine, popped it in the oven, went skiing and completely forgot about it. That night she served up the blackened terrine ceremoniously on a plate, topped with a small Union Jack and labelled 'Joan of Arc Pâté'.

CAMEMBERT SURPRISE

1 round of Camembert – about 225 g (8 oz)
225 g (8 oz) frozen puff pastry, defrosted

1 beaten egg
4 tomatoes
1 lettuce

(serves 8)

Roll out pastry very thinly into a large circle, and place the Camembert in the centre. Fold the sides of the pastry into the middle of the cheese, and pinch together. Decorate with left-over pastry and brush with beaten egg. Cook in a pre-heated, hot oven (450°F, 230°C, gas 8) for about 10–15 minutes. Serve in slices on side plates lined with lettuce. Garnish with slices of tomato.

Chalet girl comment: This is very easy to prepare and always get a gasp!

TARTE A L'OIGNON

225 g (8 oz) frozen puff pastry, defrosted
Filling
3 large onions
30 ml (2 tablespoons) butter
1 egg + 1 yolk

150 ml (¼ pint) double cream
pinch of nutmeg
salt and white pepper

(serves 6)

Line a flan ring with the pastry and chill. Slice the onions finely and cook them in the butter until soft. Beat the egg and yolk and cream together, and then stir this mixture into the onions. Season with salt, white pepper and the nutmeg, to taste. Pour into the prepared flan ring and cook in a pre-heated, moderately hot oven (400°F, 200°C, gas 6) for about 30 minutes, or until firm and golden-brown. Serve hot from the oven or cold with a nice fresh green salad.

Chalet girl comment: This dish is good for vegetarians, and is nutritious. It can be served hot, warm or cold – and can be taken on a picnic, so it is a good practical meal, as well as being delicious.

DEEP-FRIED MUSHROOMS WITH GARLIC MAYONNAISE

450 g (1 lb) button mushrooms
125 g (4 oz) flour
4 beaten eggs
oil for deep-frying
125 g (4 oz) white breadcrumbs
120 ml (8 tablespoons) mayonnaise

1 clove garlic, crushed, or 2.5 ml (½ teaspoon) garlic salt
lemon wedges and parsley for garnish

(serves 8)

Trim stems of mushrooms and wash. Roll the mushrooms in flour, then egg, and finally breadcrumbs. Deep fry in hot oil until golden. Stir garlic or garlic salt into the mayonnaise, and serve separately. Garnish the mushrooms with wedges of lemon and sprigs of parsley.

BL Chalet Girl garnish
Parsley and other herbs keep very well if stored in the fridge in a sealed plastic bag.

DEEP-FRIED CAMEMBERT

450 g (1 lb) Camembert
4 beaten eggs
125 g (4 oz) flour
225 g (8 oz) breadcrumbs

for the apricot sauce
120 ml (8 tablespoons) apricot jam

50 g (2 oz) finely chopped peanuts (or almonds)
oil for deep frying

5 ml (1 teaspoon) ground ginger

(serves 8)

Cut the Camembert into 16 equal pieces. Mix breadcrumbs and nuts together on a tray. Coat each piece of cheese with flour, then egg, and finally the nut and breadcrumb mixture. Put the finished pieces back on the tray and into the fridge, and allow coating to harden for approximately 1 hour. Repeat coating a second time – but this time don't use any flour – then deep fry in hot oil until golden-brown. Serve on shredded lettuce with apricot sauce handed separately. To make the sauce, simply melt the jam with the ginger in a saucepan until piping hot.

PEAR VINAIGRETTE

8 pears (ripe Comice or conference)
225 g (8 oz) Stilton

300 ml (½ pint) vinaigrette (see p.104)

(serves 8)

Cut the cheese into thin slices. Peel and core the pears. Slice the pears lengthways into strips, and arrange slithers of Stilton in between. Pour the vinaigrette over the pears and serve them with hot French bread.

One chalet was full of members of a rugby club, and it shook every night with their rowdy goings-on. One night after much alcohol was consumed, they took it into their heads to have a naked diving contest – off the balcony into a huge snowdrift. One of the largest and rowdiest picked himself up and rushed round, pink and naked, to the front door to go back in and have another turn. That's when he came face to face with the chalet owner. It's impossible to tell who was the more shocked.

STUFFED AUBERGINES

4 even-sized aubergines
120 ml (8 tablespoons) cooking oil
2 medium onions, finely chopped
2 cloves garlic, crushed
4 large ripe tomatoes, peeled, seeded and diced
125 g (4 oz) cooked ham, finely chopped

120 ml (8 tablespoons) cream
5 ml (1 teaspoon) Herbes de Provence
25 g (1 oz) butter
225 g (8 oz) Cheddar cheese, grated
salt and pepper

(serves 8)

Cut off stem end of aubergines and halve lengthways. Make three cuts in each half, but do not pierce the skin. Sprinkle well with salt and leave upside down to drain for 30 minutes. Rinse and dry well. Pour the oil into a large frying pan. When hot, place aubergines in, cut side down, and cook for 8 minutes, turning once or twice. Drain on kitchen paper and when cool scrape out the flesh carefully and chop. Fit the skins into an ovenproof dish. Melt the butter and cook the onions and garlic gently until soft. Stir in the aubergine flesh, tomatoes, ham, cream, and herbs, and season to taste. Fill the skins with this mixture. Sprinkle with the cheese and brown well under the grill, or bake in a moderate oven (350°C, 180°C, gas 4) for about 20 minutes.

BL Chalet Girl garnish
Put a tiny piece of parsley on each butter dish on the table.

MEXICAN RED PEPPER SOUP

50 g (2 oz) diced bacon
30 ml (2 tablespoons) oil
125 g (4 oz) chopped onion
25 g (1 oz) butter
125 g (4 oz) diced celery
125 g (4 oz) diced potato
125 g (4 oz) diced red pepper
1.25 ml (¼ teaspoon) dried thyme

600 ml (1 pint) dry white wine
1 litre (2 pints) chicken stock
125 g (4 oz) fresh tomatoes
   (skinned and chopped)
300 ml (½ pint) single cream
4 egg yolks
salt and pepper

(serves 8)

Cook the bacon and onion in oil and butter until soft. Add the other ingredients (except for the egg yolks and cream), and simmer until the vegetables are tender. Taste and season. Before serving, mix the egg yolks with the cream and add this to the soup. Stir over gentle heat until the soup thickens slightly. Do not allow to boil.

AVOCADO LES ALLUES

4 avocados
125 g (4 oz) bacon, de-rinded and diced
30 ml (2 tablespoons) oil
4 slices of white bread

90 ml (6 tablespoons) mayonnaise
30 ml (2 tablespoons) sweet vinaigrette (see p.104)

(serves 8)

Halve the avocados and remove the stones. Fry bacon in the oil until brown and crisp. Cut bread into 1 cm (½ in) cubes, and fry in the same oil until golden. Combine mayonnaise and sweetened vinaigrette, add bacon and croûtons. Fill the avocado halves, and serve on a bed of shredded lettuce.

PANSANELLA

125 g (4 oz) left-over bread (without crusts)
1 large onion
225 g (8 oz) tomatoes

1 large green pepper, de-seeded
1 cucumber
200 g (7 oz) tin of tuna, drained
vinaigrette dressing (see p.104)

(serves 6)

Break the left-over bread into chunks, and sprinkle with enough water to moisten. Squeeze out any excess water. Finely chop all the vegetables and mix with the bread. Flake the tuna and add it to the mixture. Add vinaigrette dressing to taste. Chill well and sprinkle with parsley before serving.

Chalet girl comment: Wet bread may sound awful but this is delicious – like Salade Niçoise.

COURGETTE CANOES WITH BACON AND TOMATO

8 large courgettes
2 medium onions
750 g (1¾ lb) tin of tomatoes
60 ml (4 tablespoons) tomato purée
350 g (12 oz) bacon, de-rinded
50 g (2 oz) butter
225 g (8 oz) finely grated Cheddar (or equivalent)

45 ml (3 tablespoons) fresh basil, or 10 ml (2 teaspoons) dried
30 ml (2 tablespoons) brown sugar
1 glass red wine
salt and pepper

(serves 8)

Cut the stalks off the courgettes, lie them lengthways, and slice off the top. Scrape out the centre panel of flesh, being careful not to break the skin, leaving a firm canoe shape. Blanch the canoes in plenty of boiling, salted water for 2–3 minutes. Remove and refresh under cold water. Chop onions and soften in the butter. Add the bacon, chopped, and brown lightly. Add tinned tomatoes, tomato purée, wine and sugar. Cook over medium heat for 15 minutes, and then season to taste. Remove from the heat and add the basil and the chopped courgette centres. Arrange the canoes on a serving dish, fill with the mixture, and sprinkle the cheese on top. Cook in a pre-heated moderately hot oven (400°F, 200°C, gas 6) for 25–30 minutes.

BL Chalet Girl kitchen planner tip
Make sure your knives are hanging up safely, or all facing the same way in a drawer.

HERB BREAD

1 long loaf French bread
herbs (preferably fresh), for example:
30 ml (2 tablespoons) parsley
10 ml (2 teaspoons) basil

150 ml (¼ pint) oil
125 g (4 oz) butter

10 ml (2 teaspoons) tarragon

Cut bread into slices, taking care not to sever right through. Place all the other ingredients in a saucepan, and heat gently until the butter has melted. Put the bread on a piece of tin foil large enough to enclose it completely. Using a spoon, pour some of the melted butter mixture onto each slice of bread, and the remainder over the top. Close the foil loosely over the bread and bake in a pre-heated moderately hot oven (350°–400°F, 180°–200°C, gas 4–6) for 20 minutes, or until heated through.

Chalet girl comment: The oil makes this an economical recipe, and you can prepare it all well in advance.

GARLIC BREAD

1 long (or 2 small) French loaves *2 cloves of crushed garlic*
225 g (8 oz) butter *salt and pepper*

(serves 8)

Melt butter with the crushed garlic and seasoning in a small saucepan over a low heat. Cut slices in the bread, almost all the way through, calculating two slices per person. Using a teaspoon, or a pastry brush, dribble a little of the garlic butter onto each slice of bread. Wrap the bread loosely in tin foil and cook in a pre-heated, slow oven (325°F, 170°C, gas 3) for 10–15 minutes.

CROUTONS

Cut crustless bread into 1 cm (½ in) squares and fry or deep fry until light brown and crisp, then drain well on paper. These can be done in large quantities and stored in air-tight containers. Warm through in the oven before serving.

MAIN COURSES

'Obviously, a pork chop is a pork chop, but the difference between a pork chop that is succulent and juicy and one that is cooked to a fibrous, colourless mouthful of blotting paper is the difference between good and bad cooking. Similarly, the pork chop that arrives on a cold plate straight from the kitchen is a very different pork chop from the one that arrives with the others on a large, well-decorated and laid-out dish and is served, at the table, on to sparkling clean and piping hot plates.' *The Bladon Lines Chalet Girl Manual*

SPINACH AND RICOTTA GRATIN

900 g (2 lbs) minced beef
2 large tins tomatoes
600 ml (1 pint) beef stock
tabasco
450 g (1 lb) Ricotta cheese
nutmeg
25 g (1 oz) butter
150 g (6 oz) Parmesan, grated
salt and pepper

(serves 8–10)

60 ml (4 tablespoons) oil
60 ml (4 tablespoons) tomato
  purée
4 cloves garlic, crushed with salt
tomato chili sauce (optional)
450 (1 lb) frozen chopped
  spinach, thawed and drained
150 g (6 oz) fresh breadcrumbs
4 eggs

Sauté the mince in the oil until beginning to brown. Gradually add the tinned tomatoes and juice, tomato purée and stock. Add the garlic and tabasco (to taste) and season with salt and pepper. Simmer for 1½ hours. The meat sauce should taste nicely piquant. Add tomato chili sauce if you have it. Add extra stock during the cooking if the sauce becomes too dry. Melt the butter, add the spinach, and nutmeg to taste. Cook until completely dry. Put the spinach in a bowl with the Ricotta and add the crumbs and Parmesan. Mix well and bind with the beaten eggs. Shape into golfball-sized spheres. Take the fat off the sauce, and put half the sauce in a shallow casserole. Place the cheese and spinach balls on top – but not too close together, as they expand. Top with the rest of the sauce, cover the casserole with a lid or foil, and bake for about an hour in a pre-heated, moderate oven (350°F, 180°C, gas 4), until the balls are firm.

Chalet girl comment: Good mountain food on a cold day: delicious, homely, ethnic and earthy!

FILLET OF BEEF EN CROUTE

900 g (2 lbs) fillet of beef
25 g (1 oz) beef dripping
350 g (12 oz) puff pastry
125 g (4 oz) mushrooms, sliced

25 g (1 oz) butter
125 g (4 oz) chicken liver pâté
1 beaten egg
salt and pepper

(serves 6)

Skin and trim the fillet and season well. Melt the dripping in a roasting pan, and brown the fillet on all sides until golden brown. Separately, fry the mushrooms in butter for 1 minute. When cool, mix the mushrooms with the pâté. Roll out the pastry so that it is big enough to enclose the meat, and trim the edges. Spread the pâté down the centre of the pastry, and put the joint on top (with its trussing string removed). Wrap the pastry round the joint, and seal the edges with beaten egg. Put the joint on a wet baking sheet, and brush with beaten egg. Cut the pastry trimmings into triangles, and arrange on top of the pastry. Brush with beaten egg once more. Roast the joint in a pre-heated, moderately hot oven (425°F, 220°C, gas 7) for 20 minutes, until the pastry is deep golden. This will give you rare beef. If you want the meat well done, then roast it for 15 minutes before wrapping it in the pastry.

KITZBUHEL CREAMED BEEF

1.25 kg (2¾ lbs) beef, cut into small cubes
15 ml (1 tablespoon) oil
300 ml (½ pint) water
1 beef stock cube

10 ml (2 teaspoons) cornflour
225 g (8 oz) noodles
300 ml (½ pint) soured cream
5 ml (1 teaspoon) dill
salt and pepper

(serves 6)

Brown the beef in the oil. Stir in the water, stock cube and dill, and season with salt and pepper. Cover and simmer for 1¾–2 hours. Cook the noodles and place on a dish. Put the beef on top, reserving the juices, and keep warm. Thicken the juices with the cornflour (mixed to a paste in a little water), cook for 5 minutes, and add the soured cream. Then pour over the beef and noodles.

While a chalet girl in Méribel was cleaning the downstairs rooms, she heard her colleague upstairs give a blood-curdling scream. She ran upstairs to find that the other girl had discovered a disembodied wooden leg under the bed she was making.

The guest in question was out skiing with one wooden leg on, but he had brought a spare!

MOUSSAKA

6 aubergines
4 large onions, finely sliced
900 g (2 lbs) minced beef
4 cloves garlic, crushed
2 x 750 g (1¾ lb) tin tomatoes
60 ml (4 tablespoons) tomato purée

60 ml (4 tablespoons) chicken stock
90 ml (6 tablespoons) oil
10 ml (2 teaspoons) ground cinnamon
salt and pepper

topping
4 large eggs
225 g (8 oz) cottage cheese (sieved)

300 ml (10 fl oz) single cream

(serves 8)

Remove the stem ends from the augergines and cut into slices. Sprinkle well with salt and leave for 15 minutes. Rinse in cold water and dry well. Heat half the oil in a large shallow pan. Quickly fry the slices on each side. Remove and drain on kitchen paper. Add remaining oil to pan, heat and cook onions till soft and golden. Stir in the beef and brown lightly. Season with salt and pepper and cinnamon. Mix in the tomatoes, garlic, purée and stock. Cook for 15 minutes. Layer the aubergine slices and meat sauce into a deep, ovenproof dish, finishing with aubergines. Beat together the topping ingredients, season, and pour over the dish. Bake for 45 minutes in a pre-heated, moderately hot oven (375°F, 190°C, gas 5) until the top is golden.

CHILI CON CARNE

675 g (1½ lbs) minced beef
30 ml (2 tablespoons) oil
2 diced onions
1 clove garlic
750 g (1¾ lb) tin tomatoes
2 x 400 g (14 oz) tins red kidney beans, drained
(serves 6)

chili powder
tabasco
Worcester sauce
paprika
salt and pepper

Fry the onion in the oil until soft, then add the mince and cook, stirring, until the mince has separated into little granules. Add the tomatoes and juice, the garlic, and the chili, tabasco, Worcester sauce and paprika – carefully – to taste. Season with salt and pepper. Simmer gently for about ½ hour. Add the kidney beans, and simmer for a further 15 minutes. Serve with crisp brown bread and a nice green side salad.

Chalet girl comment: This dish is great on a cold day! It freezes well, but put in less chili powder if you do freeze it – it tastes much sharper once defrosted.

CHEESY BEEF ROLLS

900 g (2 lbs) stewing steak, cut into thin slices
175 g (6 oz) Edam cheese, grated
45 ml (3 tablespoons) tomato purée
4 garlic cloves, crushed

250 ml (8 fl oz) red wine
10 ml (2 teaspoons) cornflour
1 small carton soured cream
basil (if fresh) or chopped, fresh parsley
salt and pepper

(serves 6-8)

Mix the tomato purée with the garlic. Add salt and pepper and basil to taste. Flatten the slices of beef and spread each slice with this mixture. Press the grated cheese onto this and roll each slice of beef up tightly. Secure with toothpicks and pack closely in a shallow ovenproof dish. Pour over the wine, and add enough water to come ¾ of the way up the sides of the beef rolls. Cover with foil, and put in a pre-heated moderate oven (350°F, 180°C, gas 4) for 2–2½ hours, until tender. Pour off the juices into a separate pan, and thicken with cornflour (mixed with a little water). Pour back over the beef, and top with soured cream to serve.

BL Chalet Girl kitchen planner tip
Always unwrap meat, but keep it covered on the bottom shelf of the fridge so it doesn't drip onto dairy products etc.

VEAL VAL D'ISERE

8 veal escalopes, flattened lightly
30 ml (2 tablespoons) oil
25 g (1 oz) margarine or butter
300 ml (½ pint) double cream

90 ml (6 tablespoons) cooking brandy
450 g (1 lb) button mushrooms, sliced
salt and pepper

(serves 8)

Season the escalopes, and then fry them in the oil, with the margarine or butter, until brown on each side. Remove from the pan, and place them in an ovenproof dish. Cover, and keep in a warm place while you make the sauce. Heat up the juices in the pan, add the brandy and mushrooms, and flame. When the flame dies down, add the cream, and season. Pour the sauce over the veal, and garnish with tomato wedges and a sprig of parsley.

VEAL CHIGNONS IN TOMATO SAUCE

2.5 kg (5½ lbs) minced veal
½ bottle red wine
2 beaten eggs
2 large onions
3 cloves garlic

125 g (4 oz) soft white breadcrumbs
fines herbes to taste (parsley, tarragon, chervil), chopped
salt and pepper

sauce
750 g (1¾ lb) tin tomatoes
3 onions, chopped
1 clove garlic, crushed

15 ml (1 tablespoon) oil
10 ml (2 teaspoons) brown sugar

(serves 12)

Chop the onions and garlic and combine with the minced veal, breadcrumbs, eggs, herbs and seasoning. Shape into patties (2 each), and place in a greased dish with the red wine. Cook for 40 minutes in a moderately hot oven (400°F, 200°C, gas 6). Turn once during cooking.
For the sauce: Sauté the onions and garlic in the oil until soft. Add the tomatoes, the sugar, and the wine from cooking the meat.

Season with salt and pepper, and simmer for 10 minutes. Then liquidise in the blender. Serve the chignons on top of the sauce – nouvelle cuisine-style.

Chalet girl comment: This is cheap, easy and popular party food – what else do you need?

VEAL WITH ASPARAGUS

8 veal escalopes
2 x 400g (14 oz) tins of asparagus
50 g (2 oz) butter
50 g (2 oz) flour
450 ml (¾ pint) chicken stock

150 ml (¼ pint) dry white wine
juice of ½ lemon
tarragon
oil for frying
salt and pepper

(serves 8)

Melt the butter and add the flour. Cook for 3 minutes. Gradually stir in the stock and wine, and cook for 10 minutes. Add the lemon juice and tarragon and salt and pepper to taste. Drain the asparagus, reserve 4 spears, and purée the rest. Add this purée to the sauce. Fry the veal in oil until cooked. Arrange on a serving dish, and cover with the sauce. Quickly fry the remaining asparagus tips in a little extra butter, and garnish the veal with them.

One customer dropped her children off at their ski class before hurrying to her own and consequently arrived rather late. The ski instructor, who got away with being rather caustic with his pupils because he was so dishy, reprimanded her sharply. 'Vy are you so late?' he rapped out. 'Vot do you think this is – a holiday or something?'

CHICKEN PROVENCAL

8 chicken quarters
300 ml (½ pint) dry white wine
salt and pepper

sauce
400 g (14 oz) medium tin tomatoes
4 cloves crushed garlic
10 ml (2 teaspoons) dried mixed herbs)
30 ml (2 tablespoons) tomato purée
(serves 8)

10 ml (2 teaspoons) dried tarragon
25 g (1 oz) butter, melted

2 large onions, chopped
225 g (8 oz) button mushrooms, cleaned and sliced
10 stoned green olives
10 stoned black olives
15 ml (1 tablespoon) oil
fresh parsley, chopped

Place chicken in a roasting tin and sprinkle with tarragon, melted butter, wine and seasoning. Cover with foil and cook in a pre-heated, moderately hot oven (400°F, 200°C, gas 6) for ¾ hour. Meanwhile, prepare the sauce. Cook the onions and garlic in the oil for 5 minutes. Liquidise the tinned tomatoes, and add to the onion mixture with the herbs, tomatoe purée, stoned olives and sliced mushrooms. Bring to the boil, then simmer for 8 minutes or so. When the chicken is cooked, strain the juices into the sauce. Place the chicken in a deep serving dish. Cover with the sauce, and sprinkle with chopped parsley.

BL Chalet Girl economy tip
Save scraps of left-over meat and poultry over the week. If you have enough, you can mince them and make a terrine, or put the scraps in soup.

CHICKEN AND PINEAPPLE CASSEROLE

8 chicken quarters
30 ml (2 tablespoons) oil
4 medium onions
1 tube of tomato purée
2 cloves of garlic
450 g (1 lb) tin pineapple pieces
10 ml (2 teaspoons) rosemary
2 bay leaves
1 medium tin pimentos, drained and chopped
2 green peppers, de-seeded
350 g (12 oz) mushrooms, cleaned
salt and pepper

(serves 8)

Brown the chicken pieces in the oil in a casserole. Take them out and set aside, then brown the chopped onions, garlic, peppers and mushrooms. Replace the chicken pieces, and add the pimentos and tomato purée. Pour over the contents of the tin of pineapple, and add the bay leaves and rosemary and season well. Stir all together, cover and cook slowly for 2 hours. Serve with boiled rice and salad.

LEMON HONEY CHICKEN

8 chicken breasts
90 ml (6 tablespoons) clear honey
90 ml (6 tablespoons) butter
juice of 3 lemons

(serves 8)

Place chicken pieces in a roasting tin, and season with salt and pepper. Melt the honey, butter and lemon juice in a pan over low heat. Spoon over the chicken. Cook in a pre-heated moderate oven (375°F, 190°C, gas 5) for ¾ hour, or until golden brown. Garnish with lemon twists and watercress.

Language can be a problem with new chalet girls having to cope in a foreign country for the first time. One girl rang up the cash-and-carry shop in Val d'Isère and ordered 20 chicken pieces – or so she thought. The order was delivered while she was out skiing, and she returned to find 20 whole chickens waiting on the doorstep.

SPICED CHICKEN

4 lb (2 kg) oven-ready chicken
2.5 ml (½ teaspoon) ground cloves
45 ml (3 tablespoons) tomato purée
10 ml (2 teaspoons) ground cardamom
1.25 ml (¼ teaspoon) chili powder

cucumber salad
1 large cucumber, diced
pinch of dried dill

rice pilaff
450 g (1 lb) Uncle Ben's rice
1½ litres (1½ pints) stock
2 medium onions, sliced

(serves 6)

grated rind and juice of ½ lemon
4 cloves garlic, crushed
2.5 ml (½ teaspoon) salt
5 ml (1 teaspoon) ground ginger
5 ml (1 teaspoon) ground coriander
30 ml (2 tablespoons) oil

300 ml (½ pint) soured cream
salt

2 red peppers, de-seeded and sliced
15 ml (1 tablespoon) oil
50 g (2 oz) butter

Remove skin from the chicken. Mix all the other ingredients together. Remove trussing from the chicken, and place in an ovenproof dish. Spread the spice mixture all over the chicken. Cover, and leave overnight in the refrigerator. Cook the chicken in a pre-heated moderately hot oven (400°F, 200°C, gas 6), on the shelf above centre, for 1¼ hours, until the surface is crisp and red. Serve with cucumber salad, made by mixing cucumber, cream and dill with salt. Also serve with pilaff, made by cooking the rice in the stock, and mixing with the onions and peppers, which have been fried in the oil. Finally stir in the butter with a fork.

CORONATION CHICKEN

2 medium onions, chopped
2 dessert apples, cored, peeled and chopped
20 ml (4 teaspoons) curry powder
10 ml (2 teaspoons) flour
5 ml (1 teaspoon) lemon juice
2 small chickens, poached in barely enough water to cover
50 g (2 oz) butter
300 ml (½ pint) stock from poaching the chicken
30 ml (2 tablespoons) apricot jam
90 ml (6 tablespoons) single cream
600 ml (1 pint) mayonnaise, preferably home-made
salt and pepper
paprika

(serves 8)

Fry the onion and apple together in the butter. Add the curry powder and flour, and cook for one minute. Gradually add the chicken stock, and cook until it thickens. Stir in the apricot jam, cream and lemon juice and allow to cool. Then liquidise. Remove the chicken meat from the bone. Combine the curry sauce with the mayonnaise, and stir into the chicken. Check the seasoning. Arrange on a flat serving dish and sprinkle with paprika. You can serve this with rice salad, arranged round the outer edge of the dish.

CLARMONT TURKEY

8 turkey breasts
225 g (8 oz) Boursin cheese
600 ml (1 pint) dry white wine
30 ml (2 tablespoons) double cream
salt and pepper

(serves 8)

Beat the turkey breasts flat, season and put a little of the Boursin on top of each. Roll them up, and secure with a toothpick. Simmer for 40 minutes in the white wine. Remove the turkey when cooked, and reduce the wine by half, then add the cream, check seasoning and serve.

Chalet girl comment: The only problem with this is trying to explain to a shop full of French butchers exactly which bit of the turkey you want and having to resort to mime: no, not *thighs* but *breasts* !

COURCHEVEL QUAIL

8 quail, rinsed inside and out and dried
900 g (2 lbs) cheapest (or home-made) pork-based pâté
8 slices bacon, de-rinded
60 ml (4 tablespoons) redcurrant jelly

600 ml (1 pint) unsweetened orange juice
30 ml (2 tablespoons) dry white wine
2 chicken stock cubes

(serves 8)

Stuff each bird with 125 g (4 oz) of the pâté (it *will* go in!) Wrap a slice of bacon around each one, and place on a baking sheet. Pour the orange juice round the birds, add the redcurrant jelly, the wine, and crumble in the stock cubes. All this can be done well in advance of cooking. Cover with foil and bake in a hot oven (400°F, 200°C, gas 6) for approximately 40 minutes, removing the foil 10 minutes before the end of cooking time. The birds should be served on a round of fried bread, with the juices handed separately, as gravy. You can thicken these if you wish. Also serve roast potatoes and Brussels sprouts.

BL Chalet Girl garnish
Lemon slices with chicken or veal dishes look nice and fresh.

CHICKEN CHICHELEY

6 chicken breasts
25 g (1 oz) butter
15 ml (1 tablespoon) oil
1 kg (2 lbs 4 oz) broccoli, trimmed and washed
275 g (10 oz) tin condensed cream of mushroom soup
150 g (6 oz) tin evaporated milk

300 ml (½ pint) mayonnaise
125 g (4 oz) grated Cheddar cheese
curry powder to taste
juice of ½ lemon
50 g (2 oz) crispy breadcrumbs
salt and pepper

(serves 6)

Cook chicken in the butter and oil until tender. Cook broccoli in a little boiling salted water for 5 minutes, or until half-cooked. Drain the broccoli, and arrange in a casserole. Place the chicken on top. In a separate pan, put the soup, the evaporated milk, mayonnaise, curry powder, cheese and lemon juice, and season with salt and pepper. Heat through until the cheese melts, then pour over the chicken and broccoli. Scatter the breadcrumbs over the dish and cook in a pre-heated, moderate oven (400°F, 200°C, gas 6) for 30 minutes. Serve with baked potatoes and salad.

FRENCH-FRIED CHICKEN

8 chicken quarters, skinned
60 ml (4 tablespoons) English mustard
60 ml (4 tablespoons) Dijon mustard

4 eggs, beaten
125 g (4 oz) flour
175 g (6 oz) fresh breadcrumbs
salt and pepper

(serves 8)

Season the flour, and roll the chicken pieces in it. Blend the mustards with the eggs until smooth. Dip the chicken pieces in the mustard mix and then roll them in the breadcrumbs. Ideally, put in the fridge for 8 hours, so that the mustard flavours the meat. To cook, place on an oiled baking tray, and bake for an hour in a pre-heated moderate oven (400°F, 200°C, gas 6) until the chicken is cooked.

MANGO CHICKEN

8 chicken breasts
350 g (12 oz) mango chutney
50 g (2 oz) butter

7.5 ml (1½ teaspoons) curry powder
black pepper

(serves 8)

Blend the butter with the mango chutney, add the curry powder, and season with plenty of black pepper. Skin the chicken breasts and place them in an ovenproof dish. Cover with the mango sauce, and place in a pre-heated moderate oven (375°F, 190°C, gas 5) for ¾ hour.

All chalet girls know to keep their wines under close guard so that over-enthusiastic guests don't help themselves outside dinner time. But the chalet girls of Val d'Isère were unprepared for the teetotal sneak thief who made daring raids on the orange juice, once carrying off 36 cartons from a well-stocked chalet – while completely ignoring the bottles of booze.

LUCREZIA SPECIAL

2 small pre-cooked chickens, skinned and cut into small pieces
175 g (6 oz) pre-cooked pasta shells
2 onions
15 ml (1 tablespoon) oil
15 ml (1 tablespoon) flour
125 g (4 oz) mushrooms, cleaned and chopped
½ green pepper, de-seeded and chopped
½ red pepper, de-seeded and chopped
25 g (1 oz) butter
175 g (6 oz) tin sweetcorn, drained
600 ml (1 pint) milk
dry white wine to taste
175 g (6 oz) breadcrumbs
175 g (6 oz) Cheddar cheese, grated
salt and pepper

(serves 6–8)

Chop the onions and place in a saucepan with the oil, and cook for a few minutes. Add the flour, cook for 3 minutes then gradually blend in the milk. Meanwhile, cook the mushrooms and the peppers in butter until soft. Drain off the fat, and add the vegetables to the onion sauce. Add the chicken pieces and sweetcorn, and season well. Don't forget the wine to taste – and have a glass yourself! Place this mixture in a dish, and cover with pasta shells. Mix the grated cheese and breadcrumbs together and sprinkle over the top. Place in a pre-heated moderate oven (400°F, 200°C, gas 6) for 40 minutes.

CHICKEN AND CELERY CHANCARD

6 boneless chicken breasts, cooked
2 small cartons natural yoghurt
60 ml (4 tablespoons) mayonnaise
2 onions
4 sticks celery, chopped
1 green pepper, de-seeded and chopped
1 large bag plain crisps
175 g (6 oz) Cheddar, grated
salt and pepper

(serves 8)

Chop chicken into bite-sized pieces and put in a large bowl. Add the yoghurt, mayonnaise, and the celery and chopped pepper. Then add the onion, very finely chopped (and fried for a minute or two if you prefer). Season. Mix thoroughly, and put into a casserole. Put the crisps and cheese into a blender so that they make crunchy crumbs, and then scatter them over the casserole. Put in a pre-heated moderate oven (350°F, 180°C, gas 4) for ½ hour until hot through (do not over-heat). Then flash the casserole under the grill for 2–3 minutes to brown the crispy topping.

POULET A LA VALLEE D'AUGE

6 chicken quarters
30 ml (2 tablespoons) seasoned flour
15 ml (1 tablespoon) oil
2 onions

4 cooking apples
150 ml (¼ pint) white wine
300 ml (½ pint) chicken stock
30 ml (2 tablespoons) soured cream

(serves 6)

Turn the chicken in seasoned flour and fry until golden brown. Take the pieces out, and put in a casserole. Chop the onions and apples and fry them gently until cooked. Add the stock and wine to this mixture and simmer for 2 minutes. Pour this sauce over the chicken. Put the casserole in a pre-heated slow oven (250°F, 170°C, gas 3) for 1½ hours. Just before serving check the seasoning and add the soured cream. Serve with rice.

BL Chalet Girl kitchen planner tip
Line underneath the rings of your cooker, grill and oven with tin foil. This makes cleaning very much easier.

CREAMED CHICKEN AND AVOCADO

3 small cooked chickens
3 avocados, peeled and stoned
75 g (3 oz) butter
75 g (3 oz) flour
450 ml (¾ pint) chicken stock
300 ml (½ pint) milk
150 ml (¼ pint) double cream
15 ml (1 tablespoon) dry sherry
50 g (2oz) Cheddar cheese, grated
juice of 1 lemon

(serves 8–10)

Melt the butter and add the flour. Stir in the stock, milk, and cream, and cook for 10 minutes. Take the chicken meat off the bones, and cut into bite-sized pieces, then add to the sauce. Add the sherry, and season to taste. Lay slices of avocado on the bottom of a casserole. Sprinkle with the lemon juice, and spoon the chicken mixture on top. Sprinkle with the grated cheese and bake for 45 minutes in a pre-heated moderate oven (350°F, 180°C, gas 4) until bubbling. Serve with jacket potatoes and salad.

POULET NORMANDE

8 chicken quarters, skinned
2 onions, chopped
8 slices bacon, de-rinded and chopped
4 apples, peeled, cored and chopped
80 g (3 oz) butter
125 g (4 oz) flour
600 ml (1 pint) cider
300 ml (½ pint) double cream
thyme
salt and pepper

(serves 8)

Simmer the chicken portions in the cider until cooked. Fry the onions, apples and bacon in the butter until soft. Add the flour and cook for 2 minutes, then slowly add the cider to make a roux. Add the cream, and thyme, salt and pepper to taste. Add the chicken portions to the sauce, heat through and serve.

In one of the smartest chalets in Val d'Isère the very meticulous and fussy owner lived above the Bladon Lines accommodation. She was constantly inspecting the chalet for cleanliness and tidiness. Such a martinet was she that when the rep came to visit the chalet girl, he used to walk into the chalet backwards; then if Madame La Propriétaire popped in and saw dirty footmarks she would think they belonged to a guest walking *out* of the chalet!

TIGNES TURKEY TIT-BITS

8 turkey escalopes
100 g (3½ oz) flour, seasoned with salt, pepper and tarragon
oil for frying
grated rind and juice of 3 lemons

150 ml (¼ pint) dry white wine
300 ml (½ pint) chicken stock
20 ml (4 teaspoons) dried tarragon

(serves 8)

Flour the escalopes and fry them until lightly browned on both sides. Place in an ovenproof dish. Mix the remainder of the flour with the fat in the pan. Add the wine, chicken stock, lemon juice and rind, and the rest of the tarragon. Bring to the boil, and then pour over the turkey. Bake in a pre-heated moderate oven (350°F, 180°C, gas 4) for 25 minutes. Serve garnished with lemon and parsley.

TURKEY ESCALOPES AUX CHAMPIGNONS

8 turkey escalopes
40 g (1½ oz) butter
40 g (1½ oz) flour
750 ml (1¼ pints) good chicken stock

225 g (8 oz) mushrooms, cleaned and sliced
30 ml (2 tablespoons) double cream
salt and pepper

(serves 8)

Sauté the escalopes in a little extra butter, and place in an ovenproof dish. Melt the butter in a saucepan, and add the flour off heat. Then add the chicken stock. Bring to the boil and simmer for 2 minutes, then season to taste. Add the sliced mushrooms and pour the sauce over the escalopes. Cook for 40 minutes in a pre-heated moderate oven (375°F, 190°C, gas 5). Before serving, pour over the cream and reheat gently.

POULET DE DIJON

8 chicken quarters
25 g (1 oz) butter
2 onions
225 g (8 oz) button mushrooms, cleaned
16 rashers of bacon, de-rinded

1 large clove garlic, crushed
Dijon mustard to taste
12 g (½ oz) butter
12 g (½ oz) flour
450 ml (¾ pint) milk
salt and pepper

(serves 8)

Slice the onion and sweat gently in the 25 g (1 oz) butter. Dice the bacon and add to the onions, with the garlic and mushrooms. Sweat gently for 8 minutes. Remove, and brown the chicken, adding a little extra fat if necessary. In a separate pan, melt the rest of the butter and add the flour. Add the milk, stirring continuously until thick. Add the mustard and salt and pepper to taste. Place the chicken and the vegetable mixture in a casserole, and pour the sauce over the top. Put in a pre-heated moderate oven (375°F, 190°C, gas 5) for about an hour.

BL Chalet Girl economy tip
Put all dregs of wine in a sealed bottle for cooking.

TURKEY AND HAZELNUTS

6 turkey escalopes
150 g (5 oz) chopped hazelnuts
juice of 1 lemon
600 ml (1 pint) chicken stock
50 g (2 oz) butter

50 g (2 oz) flour
75 ml (5 tablespoons) double cream
salt and pepper

(serves 6)

Fry the escalopes gently until cooked in 25 g (1 oz) butter. Keep warm in the oven. Melt the rest of the butter, and make a roux with the flour. Pour on the chicken stock, and stir continuously until it boils and thickens. Add the hazelnuts and lemon juice, and season to taste. Just before serving, add the cream, then pour over the escalopes.

Two customers turned up in Méribel late on a Saturday night, having driven out to the resort. They wandered round for a long time and finally found their chalet. They were welcomed in by the people there, none of whom they knew.

'But where are Jim and Julia?' they asked over dinner. Jim and Julia, they were told, were arriving the next day.

It wasn't until they were part of the welcoming party for Jim and Julia the next morning, that they realised something had gone wrong. The couple arrived – and they weren't the Jim and Julia the two customers knew. These were famous film actors. They hastily tracked down a rep and were directed to the chalet they should have gone to in the first place. It turned out that they had wined and dined in a private chalet full of stars of the stage and screen – none of whom they had recognised!

LEMON CHICKEN COURMAYEUR

6 large pieces of chicken, quarters or breasts
grated rind and juice of 2 lemons
2 cloves finely chopped garlic
60 ml (4 tablespoons) oil

50 g (2 oz) butter
oregano
basil
chopped parsley
salt and pepper

(serves 6)

Place the chicken in a large bowl. Mix the oil, lemon, garlic, seasoning and herbs together, and pour over the chicken. Cover and leave overnight, or all day, in the fridge to marinate. Then put the chicken in a buttered roasting tin, and pour the marinade over. Dot with butter and cook for an hour, in a pre-heated, moderately hot oven (375°F, 190°C, gas 5). Baste the chicken occasionally. Sprinkle with chopped parsley before serving, and hand the juices separately.

LAMB BOULANGERE

1 lamb chop per person, trimmed
1 onion per person
1 large potato per person, peeled

butter
stock
salt and pepper

Brown the lamb chops in a little butter. Thinly slice the potatoes. Thinly slice and blanch the onions. Butter an ovenproof dish and spread half the thinly sliced potatoes over the base. Season, and spread half the onions on top. Place all the chops on top of the onions. Put all the rest of the onions on top of the chops, and finish with a layer of potatoes. Season again. Pour over some well-flavoured stock, dot with butter and cover with foil. Cook in a pre-heated moderately hot oven (400°F, 200°C, gas 6) for 1 hour, or until tender. Remove the foil, and cook for a further ¼ of an hour, to lightly brown the top.

LAMB CUTLET LE CAIRN

8 lamb cutlets
4 chopped onions
50 g (2 oz) mushrooms, cleaned and sliced
25 g (1 oz) butter

Cumberland sauce
250 ml (8 fl oz) redcurrant jelly
juice of ½ lemon

125 g (4 oz) grated Cheddar cheese
900 g (2 lbs) puff pastry
2 beaten eggs
salt and pepper

rind and juice of 2 oranges
60 ml (4 tablespoons) port

(serves 8)

Trim the fat from the lamb cutlets. Cook the onions and mushrooms until soft in the butter and then season. Roll out the pastry thinly and cut into 8 large squares. Put one cutlet on top of each. Divide the onion and mushroom mixture between the eight cutlets, and pile a little cheese on top of this. Fold the pastry over the cutlets, and brush the top with beaten egg. Cut a slit on the top. Bake in a pre-heated hot oven (425°F, 220°C, gas 7) for 35 minutes. Serve with Cumberland sauce, which you make as follows: peel the oranges, clean the rind of pith. Cut the orange rind into thin shreds and blanch in boiling water. Drain. Warm and melt the jelly, add the juices, port and strips of rind.

Chalet girl comment: If your guests have hearty appetites you may want to give them two each.

BL Chalet Girl tip
A few grains of rice in a salt cellar will keep the salt dry.

CRUNCHY-TOPPED PORK CHOPS

8 pork chops
20 ml (4 teaspoons) dried mustard
45 ml (3 tablespoons) demerara sugar
50 g (2 oz) chopped salted peanuts

10 ml (2 teaspoons) Worcester sauce
10 ml (2 teaspoons) wine vinegar
5 ml (1 teaspoon) salt
10 ml (2 teaspoons) melted butter

(serves 8)

Grill the chops until nearly cooked. Mix all the other ingredients together, and spread over the chops. Return to the grill and cook until golden brown.

SPACE SUIT PORKIES

8 pork chops
12 g (½ oz) butter
10 ml (2 teaspoons) oil
120 ml (8 tablespoons) soured cream

225 g (8 oz) mushrooms, cleaned and sliced
pinch of fresh or dried marjoram, thyme and sage
salt and pepper

(serves 8)

Brown the chops in the butter and oil, but do not cook through. Put each chop on a square of foil, large enough to enclose it totally. Season. Mix the mushrooms, herbs and soured cream, and spoon a little on top of each chop. Close the foil *loosely* over the chops and cook for 20–30 minutes in a pre-heated, moderately hot oven (400°F, 200°C, gas 6). Place each chop on a plate, still in its 'space suit', and garnish the foil with a wedge of tomato and a sprig of parsley.

Chalet girl comment: If the foil wrapping is too tight the chop will not cook through properly.

DIJON ROAST PORK

900 g (2 lb) rolled joint of roasting pork
60 ml (4 tablespoons) Dijon mustard
30 ml (2 tablespoons) red wine vinegar

apple sauce
600 ml (1 pint) chicken stock

10 ml (2 teaspoons) caster sugar
125 g (4 oz) soft breadcrumbs
cloves
salt and pepper

125 g (4 oz) apple purée
10 ml (2 teaspoons) cornflour

(serves 8)

Combine mustard, vinegar and sugar, and stir well. Stud the joint of pork with the cloves, and season. Spread the mustard dressing onto the joint and sprinkle with breadcrumbs. Put in a roasting tray and place in pre-heated moderate oven (375°F, 190°C, gas 5) to cook. Allow 40 minutes per pound. Remove the joint from the roasting tray, and prepare the sauce as follows: place the tray over a gentle heat, and allow the sediment to settle. Strain off the fat. Pour in the stock and stir to combine with the sediment. Add the puréed apple and bring to the boil. Mix the cornflour with a little water, and use to thicken sauce. Simmer for 5 minutes. Carve the pork into thin slices, and arrange on a flat dish. Pour a little sauce over the meat, and serve the rest separately. If you like, decorate the meat with a few fried apple rings.

In Budget Chalets there are lots of triple and four-bedded rooms. It's up to each chalet party who they put to sleep where. Sometimes it works out that boys and girls who have never met before end up sleeping in the same room. One girl was horrified to find herself put in a room with some boys, until she fell in love with the boy in the top bunk – and eventually married him.

PORK PARMESAN WITH TOMATO SAUCE

6 pork fillets, trimmed of fat
8 rashers of bacon, de-rinded
75 g (3oz) plain flour
125 g (4 oz) tin tomato purée
4 beaten eggs
2 cloves garlic
Worcester sauce
salt and pepper
3 large onions

150 g (5 oz) Parmesan cheese, grated
75 ml (5 tablespoons) oil
2 x 400 g (14 oz) tins tomatoes
150 g (5 oz) strong Cheddar, grated
mixed herbs to taste
450 ml (¾ pint) chicken stock
cayenne pepper

(serves 12)

Cut the fillets into chunks. Mix 75 g (3 oz) of the Parmesan cheese with the flour, and season with salt and pepper. Dip the pork into the beaten egg, then roll in the floor mixture. Fry in 60 ml (4 tablespoons) oil until golden brown. Meanwhile, make a tomato sauce. Chop the onions, garlic, and bacon and fry together in 15 ml (1 tablespoon) oil. When soft, add the tomatoes and juice, tomato purée, Worcester sauce, herbs and stock. Season to taste, and cook for about 10 minutes. Layer the pork and sauce in a large casserole dish. Just before adding the last layer of sauce, place all the grated Cheddar on top. Cover with the rest of the sauce, and sprinkle on the remaining Parmesan. Bake in a moderate oven (375°F, 190°C, gas 5) for 1¼ hours.

Chalet girl comment: This can be prepared in the morning. It is fairly inexpensive, and is delicious served with baked potatoes and green salad.

BL Chalet Girl kitchen planner tip
Keep a large jar filled with rice that you use just for baking pastry cases blind.

BLADON LINES GOUGERE

choux pastry
125 g (4 oz) plain flour
250 ml (8 fl oz) water
4 large eggs

pinch of salt
125 g (4 oz) butter

béchamel sauce
600 ml (1 pint) milk
piece carrot
1 bay leaf
25 g (1 oz) cornflour

1 small onion
piece celery
25 g (1 oz) butter
salt and pepper

filling
225 g (8 oz) mushrooms, cleaned and sliced
3 large tomatoes, peeled, seeded and chopped

225 g (8 oz) tin sweetcorn, drained
225 g (8 oz) ham, chopped

(serves 8)

Make the choux pastry by bringing the water to boil with the butter and salt. Add the flour and mix well. Continue to cook over a low heat until the mixture leaves the side of the pan. Allow to cool a little and beat in the eggs one at a time, until the mixture is smooth and shiny. Leave to cool, then spread (with the help of wet fingers) into and up the sides of a large ovenproof dish. Make the sauce by heating the milk with the sliced vegetables and bay leaf to boiling, then remove from the heat and allow to infuse for 5 minutes. Melt the butter and stir in the flour, mix well and cook for 3 minutes. Add the flavoured milk, and cook for a further 5 minutes. Mix in the filling ingredients and season carefully. Pour into the pastry-lined dish and bake in a pre-heated hot oven (425°F, 220°C, gas 7) for about 35 minutes, until well-risen and deep golden brown.

Chalet girl comment: A traditional Bladon Lines dish that everyone just expects to have once in a while. Very tasty and cheap to make – and it looks very nice.

PORK STROGANOFF

3 pork fillets, trimmed of fat
15 ml (1 tablespoon) oil
15 ml (1 tablespoon) butter
225 g (8 oz) cream cheese

225 g (8 oz) mushrooms, cleaned
2 large onions, chopped
½ tube tomato purée
salt and pepper

(serves 8–10)

Cut the pork fillet into bite-size strips. Fry the pieces in a mixture of oil and butter until cooked through. Remove and keep hot. Fry the mushrooms and onions in the same pan until soft. Add the cream cheese and tomato purée to this mixture, and stir until smooth and creamy. Put the meat back in the pan, mix well, and season to taste. Serve immediately.

GRANNY'S PORK CHOPS

8 pork chops
80 ml (5 tablespoons) brown sugar or honey

80 ml (5 tablespoons) Dijon or grainseed mustard

(serves 8)

Mix the mustard and sugar together, and coat the chops lavishly on each side with the mixture. Grill on both sides until tender, and the topping is crisp. When the chops are cooked, pour over any juices that have collected in the pan.

PORK AND ORANGE CHOPS

6 pork chops
1 small orange
200 ml (⅓ pint) orange juice
300 ml (½ pint) cider
15 ml (1 tablespoon) brown sugar

15 ml (1 tablespoon) mustard
oil for frying
25 g (1 oz) butter
15 ml (1 tablespoon) flour
salt and pepper

(serves 6)

Mix the mustard and sugar, and thinly coat each chop with the mixture. Heat the oil, and brown the chops. Drain away the surplus oil. In a separate pan, make the sauce by melting the butter, stirring in the flour and cooking for a minute or so. Gradually add the orange juice and cider. Season. Pour this sauce over the chops in their pan, and allow to simmer for 20 minutes. Serve decorated with orange slices.

CIDER-BAKED PORK CHOPS

8 pork chops
225 g (8 oz) mushrooms, cleaned
4 cooking apples, peeled, cored and sliced
4 onions, sliced

1.2 litres (2 pints) dry cider
225 g (8 oz) grated Cheddar cheese
125 g (4 oz) breadcrumbs
salt and pepper

(serves 8)

Butter a shallow, ovenproof dish. Place the sliced onions in the base of the dish. Season, and add the pork chops. Place the sliced apples on top of the chops, and then add the sliced mushrooms. Mix the grated cheese and breadcrumbs with the seasonings, and sprinkle over the chops. Pour round the cider, and bake in a pre-heated moderately hot oven (375°F, 190°C, gas 5) for 1¼–1½ hours, until the chops are cooked and the liquid reduced.

One night in Courmayeur the chalet girls in Budget Chalet Serena were woken up by the most terrible racket outside their bedroom at about three a.m. They rushed outside to find the corridor full of snow, and their guests skiing down it!

PORK A L'ORANGE

8 pork chops
15 ml (1 tablespoon) oil
30 ml (2 tablespoons) flour
15 ml (1 tablespoon) French mustard

15 ml (1 tablespoon) honey
600 ml (1 pint) unsweetened orange juice, from a carton
2 oranges

(serves 8)

Put the chops and oil onto a baking dish, and cook in a pre-heated moderately hot oven (400°F, 200°C, gas 6) for ½ hour, or until nearly cooked. Take the chops out of the tray and keep warm. Add the flour to the pan juices and cook for a minute or two. Add the mustard, honey, orange juice, and the grated rind of the oranges. Taste, and see if you need more mustard or honey, then cook for a further 10 minutes. Pour this sauce over the chops and garnish with some parsley, watercress and the oranges cut into slices.

Chalet girl comment: Everyone seems to adore this dish, especially if it is served with minted peas – but little do they know how easy it is to make!

PORK CHOPS GRINDELWALD

8 pork chops
50 g (2 oz) butter
4 oranges, peeled and cleaned of pith
225 g (8 oz) soft brown sugar
150 ml (¼ pint) wine vinegar

150 ml (¼ pint) orange juice
10 ml (2 teaspoons) wholegrain mustard
20 ml (4 teaspoons) cornflour
salt and pepper

(serves 8)

Trim the chops, and fry in butter until well browned on both sides. Place in an ovenproof dish. Blend together the sugar, vinegar, orange juice and mustard, and season with salt and pepper. Pour this over the chops, and then put slices of orange over the top. Cover with foil and bake in a pre-heated moderate oven (350°F, 180°C, gas 4) for ½ hour. Lift the chops and orange onto a serving dish, and keep warm. Blend the cornflour with a little water and stir into the liquid. Bring the sauce to the boil, and simmer until thickened. Pour the sauce over the chops to serve.

LOIN OF PORK WITH BLUE CHEESE

8 slices loin of pork, weighing 175 g (6 oz) each
600 ml (1 pint) chicken stock
350 g (12 oz) Stilton, or other blue cheese, crumbled
175 g (6 oz) butter

2 carrots
4 sticks celery
120 ml (8 tablespoons) double cream
salt and pepper

(serves 8)

Slice the carrots and celery into fine, julienne strips, and blanch separately in boiling, salted water. Refresh with cold water and set aside. In a heavy pan, sauté the pork pieces in 125 g (4 oz) of the butter, gently browning them on each side until cooked. Put them on a serving dish covered with foil and keep warm in the oven. Deglaze the pan juices with the stock, and reduce it for 5 minutes. Add the cheese and season with salt and pepper. Stir until the cheese dissolves. Add the cream and the rest of the butter, to give the sauce a shine. Remove the meat from the oven, spoon a little of the sauce over each piece, sprinkle with the carrot and celery, and serve. Hand the rest of the sauce separately.

BL Chalet Girl garnish
Watercress on meat dishes, such as pork chops, looks and tastes fresh. Be careful to pick the watercress over carefully.

PORK AND MUSHROOM PARCELS

6 medium leg of pork steaks
15 ml (1 tablespoon) oil
sage
225 g (8 oz) mushrooms, cleaned and sliced
6 rashers streaky bacon, de-rinded

15 ml (1 tablespoon) plain flour
150 ml (¼ pint) chicken stock
675 g (1½ lbs) frozen puff pastry
1 beaten egg
salt and pepper

(serves 6)

Fry the streaky bacon and set aside to cool. Liberally sprinkle the pork steaks with sage, and fry them in the oil, browning them on all sides evenly for about 10 minutes. Set aside to cool. Using the same frying pan (with the sage and pork-flavoured oil) fry the sliced mushrooms until cooked (about 5 minutes). Mix in the flour and cook for a further 3 minutes, then gradually stir in enough chicken stock to make the mushroom sauce quite thick but still slightly runny. Season. Spoon this sauce over each pork steak, and lay a rasher of bacon on top. Roll out the pastry and make individual parcels with the pork steaks and topping. Brush with the beaten egg and place in a pre-heated, very hot oven (450°F, 230°C, gas 8) for 15 minutes until the pastry has risen. Then reduce the oven to moderately hot (400°F, 200°C, gas 6) and cook for a further 20 minutes until golden brown.

One guest washed her smalls and hung them out to dry on her balcony. It was a lovely sunny day, and conditions were perfect for drying – or so she thought. Unfortunately she left them out all night, and when she brought them in the next morning they were completely stiff.

JO'S COD PARCELS

8 cod steaks
225 g (8 oz) mushrooms
2 large oranges
125 g (4 oz) chopped walnuts
1 large clove garlic, chopped

50 g (2 oz) butter
sage
thyme
salt and pepper

(serves 8)

Sweat the garlic in butter and add the mushrooms. Cook over a low heat for 5 minutes or so. Cut 8 pieces of foil, large enough to enclose the cod steaks loosely, and put one piece of cod in the centre of each. Put a little of the mushroom mixture on each piece of cod, sprinkle over some chopped walnuts, and top with a thick slice of orange. Put a pinch of each herb on the orange and season with salt and pepper. Enclose the fish and topping in the foil, and place in a pre-heated moderate oven (350°F, 180°C, gas 4) for about half an hour.

Chalet girl comment: This is absolutely delicious, and particularly good served with leeks in cheese sauce or a salad.

SEAFOOD CRUMBLE

450 g (1 lb) frozen fish fillet
175 g (6 oz) tin mussels
2 x 175 g (6 oz) tins prawns
crumble topping
175 g (6 oz) flour
40 g (1½ oz) butter

40 g (1½ oz) butter
40 g (1½ oz) flour
900 ml (1½ pints) milk
salt and pepper

125 g (4 oz) Cheddar cheese, grated

(serves 6)

Defrost fish and poach in the milk. When cooked, strain and reserve milk. Flake the fish, and put in an ovenproof dish with the mussels and prawns. Melt the butter, stir in the flour, and cook for 2 minutes. Add the poaching milk. Season with salt and pepper. Pour over the fish. Rub the butter into the flour until it resembles breadcrumbs, lightly stir in the cheese and scatter over the fish. Place in a moderate oven (350°F, 180°C, gas 4) for 30–45 minutes.

SEAFOOD CREPES

batter
225 g (8 oz) plain flour
2 eggs
2 egg yolks
600 ml (1 pint) milk
pinch salt
30 ml (2 tablespoons) oil

filling
1 kg (2 lbs 4 oz) white fish fillet
300 ml (½ pint) white wine
500 g (1 lb 2 oz) shelled prawns
600 ml (1 pint) thick roux
salt and pepper

(serves 12)

Process the batter ingredients in the blender for 15 seconds. Use to make crêpes, and then set aside. Poach the fish in the wine until white and flaky. Make a thick roux (using the wine if you wish) and mix in the fish and prawns. Season. Stuff each pancake with the fish mixture, and place on a baking tray. Heat the crêpes in a moderate oven (375°F, 190°C, gas 5) for 20 minutes. Serve with green salad.

Chalet girl comment: A filling and expensive-*looking* party dish, which doesn't in fact cost very much.

BL Chalet Girl convenience tip
Pre-prepared food usually costs much more, so budget-conscious chalet girls are told to avoid them. But there are some convenience foods on the approved list: puff pastry; certain frozen vegetables (only if they are not available fresh); bread and croissants; cereals; tinned tomato purée; brandy snaps; biscuits.

KIPPER AND VEGETABLE BAKE

900 g (2 lbs) carrots, scrubbed
    and lightly scraped
4 large onions
450 g (1 lb) mushrooms, cleaned
    and quartered
4 large kipper fillets

50 g (2 oz) butter
50 g (2 oz) flour
125 g (4 oz) Cheddar cheese
300 ml (½ pint) milk
salt and pepper

(serves 8)

Slice the carrots and cook for 5 minutes in boiling salted water. Strain and keep the liquid for the sauce. Slice the onions finely and fry half an onion in the butter. Add the flour to this and cook for about half a minute. Add the milk and enough of the carrot stock to make a fairly thick sauce. Season. In a large casserole, layer the carrots, raw onion and mushrooms, and chop the kipper fillets and put them on top. Pour over the sauce, and sprinkle with the grated cheese. Cover the casserole and cook in a pre-heated moderate oven (350°F, 180°C, gas 4) for 30–45 minutes.

LUIGI'S PIZZA

pizza base
300 g (10 oz) plain flour
pinch salt

75 g (3 oz) margarine
milk or water to mix

topping
2 x 400 g (14 oz) tins tomatoes
125 g (4 oz) grated cheese,
    Gruyère or Cheddar
10 slices salami

15 ml (1 tablespoon) oil
mixed herbs
salt and pepper

(serves 6)

Sift the flour and salt into a food processor, and add the chopped margarine. Mix together, and then add milk and water gradually until the mixture forms a ball. (If it becomes too wet, add more flour.) Roll the dough out to fit a round flan dish approx. 300 cm (12 in) round. Make the edges a little thicker than the middle. Bake in a pre-heated moderately hot oven (400°F, 200°C, gas 6) for 15 minutes. Strain the juice from the tomatoes. Chop the tomatoes and arrange them on the pizza base. Season lightly. Sprinkle with oil and herbs. Scatter the cheese over the top, and arrange the salami slices over this. Place in a pre-heated hot oven (450°F, 230°C, gas 8) for 10–15 minutes, until the cheese has melted.

Over the Christmas fortnight one chalet girl had the task of dealing with the appetites of a group from Sandhurst. Nothing she could do seemed to fill them up. In desperation she made stacks of sandwiches for their packed lunches, which became larger and larger each day. Unfortunately, so did the soldiers. On the last day of the holiday she knew that she had succeeded from one point of view when one of her hefty, well-fed soldiers became wedged so firmly in the chairlift seat that all chairlifts were brought to a standstill for an hour while they worked to free him.

VEGETARIAN LASAGNE

12 sheets lasagne
900 g (2 lbs) fresh tomatoes, or
 1 x 800 g (1 lb 12 oz) tin
900 g (2 lbs) mushrooms,
 cleaned and roughly chopped
4 cloves garlic
15 ml (1 tablespoon) olive oil

15 ml (1 tablespoon) sugar
marjoram to taste
150 ml (¼ pint) single cream
125 g (4 oz) grated cheese
 (Cheddar, or Cheddar and
 Parmesan mixed)
salt and pepper

(serves 6)

Cook the lasagne sheets according to directions. Fry the mushrooms gently in the oil, add the tomatoes (peeled and chopped, if fresh) and simmer for 10 minutes. Add the chopped garlic, sugar and seasonings and simmer for 5 minutes. In a wide, shallow ovenproof dish, arrange a layer of the mushroom sauce. Cover with a layer of lasagne sheets. Repeat the layers, finishing with a layer of lasagne. Pour over the cream and sprinkle with cheese. Cook for ½ hour in a pre-heated moderately hot oven (400°F, 200°C, gas 6).

VEGETABLES AND SALADS

'Vegetables require particular attention – in selection, in cooking and in presentation. Where there is a limited variety available it is best to concentrate on the spuds. Cooking potatoes is easy and cheap, but to do it well requires effort.' *The Bladon Lines Chalet Girl Manual*

PAPRIKA POTATOES

1.8 kg (4 lbs) potatoes, peeled and thinly sliced
8 onions, thinly sliced
2 x 400 g (14 oz) tins tomatoes

75 g (3 oz) grated cheese – Cheddar, preferably
30 ml (2 tablespoons) paprika
1.2 litres (2 pints) milk
salt and pepper

(serves 8)

Butter a shallow, ovenproof dish. Arrange a layer of potato in the bottom of the dish. Follow this with a layer of onion, then with tomato, then season with salt and pepper, and sprinkle with some of the paprika. Repeat the layers until all the vegetables are used up, adding a layer of potatoes last. Pour round the milk, and top with the grated cheese. Bake in a pre-heated, moderate oven (375°F, 190°C, gas 5) for 1½–2 hours, or until cooked.

ZERMATT POTATOES

1 kg (2 lbs 4 oz) scrubbed potatoes, unpeeled and sliced
45 ml (3 tablespoons) wholegrain mustard

½ litre (¾ pint) milk
1 beaten egg
5 ml (1 teaspoon) nutmeg
salt and pepper

(serves 8)

Spread the sliced potatoes in a buttered ovenproof dish in layers. Beat the other ingredients together, and season with salt and pepper. Pour this mixture over the potatoes. Bake in a pre-heated moderately hot oven (400°F, 200°C, gas 6) for 1 hour or until tender.

SAUTE POTATOES WITH BASIL

1.35 kg (3 lbs) unpeeled
  scrubbed potatoes, sliced
oil for deep frying

dried basil
salt and pepper

(serves 8)

Deep fry the potatoes in two or three batches until cooked and golden brown. Drain well and sprinkle with dried basil and seasoning.

DELMONICA POTATOES

900 g (2 lbs) unpeeled, cubed
  potatoes
300 ml (½ pint) double cream
300 ml (½ pint) milk
mixed herbs to taste
2 green peppers, de-seeded and
  diced

2 red peppers, de-seeded and
  diced
oil for frying
225 g (8 oz) grated cheese –
  Cheddar or Cheshire
salt and pepper

(serves 8)

Mix the potatoes, cream, milk and herbs together. Season to taste, and put into a roasting tin and bake for 40 minutes in a moderate oven (375°F, 190°C, gas 5). Meanwhile, lightly fry the peppers, and drain them on kitchen paper. When the potatoes are cooked, transfer them to an earthenware dish and scatter the peppers over the top. Cover with the grated cheese and brown under the grill.

PARTY BAKED POTATOES

1 large potato per person
5g (¼ oz) butter per potato

15 ml (1 tablespoon) milk per
  potato
salt and pepper

Bake the potatoes as normal. When slightly cooled, slice in half lengthways, and scoop the insides into a mixing bowl – being careful not to tear the skins. Mash with a fork, mixing in the butter and milk. Season well with salt and pepper. Refill the potato skins with this mixture, and decorate the tops with a fork. Reheat in a pre-heated moderate oven (350°F, 180°C, gas 4), and then flash the potatoes under the grill to brown the tops.

POSH BAKED POTATOES

*1 large potato per
  person*

*oil
salt and pepper*

Cut potatoes in half lengthways, and lightly score diagonal lines across them (about ½ cm (¼ in) deep). Then score lines in the opposite direction, so that you end up with a diamond pattern. Brush with a little oil and season with salt and pepper. Cook for about an hour in a pre-heated hot oven (450°F, 230°C, gas 8), until soft.

Chalet girl comment: These look very pretty, as the diamond shapes puff up and go a golden brown. It is also useful if you want to cook baked potatoes when you are short of time.

BL Chalet Girl kitchen planner tip
Line your vegetable basket or drawer with paper to stop the dirt falling through.

AMANDINES POTATOES

choux pastry

50 g (2 oz) margarine
125 g (4 oz) plain flour
4 eggs

pinch salt
300 ml (½ pint) water

potato mixture

900 g (2 lbs) potatoes
225 g (8 oz) flour
4 beaten eggs
350 g (12 oz) white breadcrumbs

125 g (4 oz) sliced almonds
salt and pepper
oil for deep frying

(serves 8)

Make the choux pastry by bringing the water to boil with the margarine and salt. Add the flour and mix well. Continue to cook over a low heat until the mixture leaves the side of the pan. Allow to cool a little and beat in the eggs one at a time, until the mixture is smooth and shiny. Cook the peeled potatoes in boiling salted water until tender, and drain well. Mash the potatoes, and add the choux pastry. Beat well with a wooden spoon. Correct the seasoning. Mix the breadcrumbs and nuts together. Roll the mashed potatoes into small balls. Pass the balls through the flour, roll them in the beaten egg, and then in the breadcrumb mixture. Deep fry in hot oil until golden brown, then drain on kitchen paper.

POTATO, ONION AND APPLE DAUPHINOISE

4 large potatoes
3 large cooking apples
3 large onions

900 ml (1½ pints) chicken stock
salt and black pepper

(serves 6)

Peel all the vegetables and fruit and core the apples. Slice them all thinly, either by hand or in a food processor. Lay the slices in layers in a large, flat ovenproof dish, and pour over the stock. Liberally season with black pepper, add salt, and cover with silver foil. Bake in a very hot oven (450°F, 230°C, gas 8) for 45 minutes. Remove the cover, and bake in a moderate oven (350°F, 180°C, gas 4) for a further 20 minutes.

Chalet girl comment: A delicious vegetable dish to serve with pork.

Preparing packed lunches is not a favourite pastime of chalet girls. Guests have to say the night before if they want one, and most do without. In one party there was a particularly persistent man who put an 'X' on the packed lunch list every day. Two of the girls decided to play a joke on him, and prepared a beautiful salami salad roll, secretly garnished with an elastic band. After dinner that night the rest of the party told the girls how hilarious it was when, after a bout of enthusiastic chomping, the band snapped upwards, slapping him across the face. Much to their surprise, the hungry guest put another 'X' on the list the next day. This time, they nestled a long piece of string in amongst the goodies in his roll and, not wanting to miss the fun, they followed the party the next day. From their hiding place they watched the determined eater munch his way through the roll, completely unaware that the string had uncoiled and was hanging limply from the filling. It wasn't till his last large mouthful that he found himself chewing perplexedly on the piece of string. He was furious, but his companions were helpless with laughter. The chalet girls were now convinced that they had won the battle of the packed lunch – till they found another 'X' on the list the next day. 'Are you *sure* you want one?' they asked demurely. 'Yes,' he replied equally innocently. 'Your fillings are always so inventive and imaginative.' Game, set and match to the customer.

LEEK AND POTATO BAKE

6 good-sized leeks – trimmed and well-washed
6 large potatoes
150 ml (¼ pint) double cream
150 ml (¼ pint) milk
125 g (4 oz) butter
salt and pepper

(serves 6)

Peel and slice potatoes thinly. Slice the leeks diagonally into pieces about 2.5 cm (1 in) long. Melt the butter in a large saucepan. Take off the heat and put in the potato and leek slices. Stir them, until they are evenly coated with the butter, and season well. Put the vegetables into a shallow, ovenproof dish. Mix the cream with the milk, and pour over the top. Add more milk if this mixture does not quite cover the vegetables. Cook in a pre-heated, moderately hot oven (400°F, 200°C, gas 6) for about 45 minutes, or until the potatoes are tender.

MASHED POTATO AND CARROT

700 g (1½ lbs) potatoes, peeled
175 g (6 oz) carrots, washed and scraped
50 g (2 oz) butter or margarine
salt and pepper

(serves 6)

Boil the potatoes and carrots until soft. Drain and mash together with the butter, and season with salt and pepper.

SPANISH-METHOD RICE

50 g (2 oz) of rice per person, and 50 g (2 oz) for the pot
oil for frying
salt

Wash well and drain the rice. Fry the rice for 1 or 2 minutes. Pour boiling water over the rice, approximately 2½ times the volume of rice. Season. Bring to the boil and simmer, stirring very occasionally. Test rice – when it is partially cooked but still nutty, turn off the heat, and cover the saucepan with a clean dishcloth. About 10 minutes later the rice will have absorbed the remaining water and be ready.

BROCCOLI BOUTON D'OR

900 g (2 lbs) broccoli
30 ml (2 tablespoons) almonds
oil for frying
salt

(serves 8)

Boil the broccoli in salted water for 8–10 minutes, or until tender. Drain. Fry almonds in a little oil, then drain on kitchen paper. Sprinkle the almonds with salt, and then scatter over the broccoli just before serving.

CARROTS IN WHITE SAUCE

900 g (2 lbs) carrots, washed
25 g (1 oz) butter or margarine
25 g (1 oz) flour
300 ml (½ pint) milk
15 ml (1 tablespoon) chopped parsley
salt and pepper

(serves 6)

Scrape the carrots and slice them into very thin rounds. Cook in boiling salted water until tender, but still crunchy – this should take between 2 and 4 minutes, depending on how thin you managed to slice them! Make a basic white sauce by melting the butter, stirring in the flour and cooking for a minute or two. Gradually stir in the milk and cook, continuing to stir, for about 8 minutes. Season well, and add the parsley. Drain the carrots and cover with the hot sauce.

LEMON-GLAZED CARROTS

900 g (2 lbs) carrots, trimmed and scrubbed
125 g (4 oz) butter
juice of 2 lemons
15 ml (1 tablespoon) sugar
salt and pepper

(serves 8)

Slice the carrots and par-boil them. Drain. Put them in a saucepan with the other ingredients, and cook until the carrots have absorbed all the butter.

LEEKS IN CHEESE SAUCE

8 leeks
50 g (2 oz) butter
75 g (3 oz) wholemeal flour
150 g (6 oz) grated cheese

10 ml (2 teaspoons) mustard
1 clove garlic, chopped
300 ml (½ pint) milk

(serves 8)

Chop the leeks into 2.5 cm (1 in) slices, and simmer in a little boiling salted water for 5 minutes. Strain, and reserve the water for the sauce. Melt the butter, and then add the flour and mustard. Stir and cook for about ½ minute. Add the chopped garlic, then the milk and enough leek water to make a thickish sauce, and season well. Cook for 5 minutes, and then add the cheese to the sauce, keeping aside a little to sprinkle on the top. Pour the sauce over the leeks, top with the remaining cheese, and put in a pre-heated moderate oven (400°F, 200°C, gas 6) for 15 minutes.

GLAZED CARROTS

900 g (2 lbs) carrots, scrubbed
   and cut into chunks

125 g (4 oz) butter
60 ml (4 tablespoons) honey

(serves 8)

Cook the carrots in boiling, salted water, for 8 minutes, or until just tender. Drain the carrots and put them back in the pan with the butter and honey. Cook gently for 5 minutes, until they are well coated with the glaze.

The directors of a well-known ski tour operating company (?!) took all the reps and chalet girls in Verbier out for lunch up the mountain one day, as an end of season treat. They all had an extremely jolly lunch and some of them overdid it slightly.

One of the chalet girls, too sloshed to ski home, was put into the bubble lift to go down to the village. Unfortunately she failed to get out at the bottom, and was rescued some hours later by the rep, still sailing round and round.

The poor customers in her chalet had to be sent out to a restaurant for dinner that night – at the company's expense!

LE TROIS VALLEES TRIO

450 g (1 lb) carrots, washed
1 head of celery, washed
225 g (8 oz) mangetouts, tipped and rinsed
25 g (1 oz) butter
salt and pepper

(serves 6)

Scrape the carrots and cut into thin strips about 6 cm (2½ in) long. Cut the celery into the same sized pieces. Boil in lightly salted water for 8 minutes and then drain. Separately, boil the mangetouts for 5 minutes and then drain. Toss all the vegetables with the butter, season, and serve immediately.

Chalet girl comment: This is a very colourful way of serving vegetables which looks faintly exotic without being expensive.

CABBAGE WITH NUTMEG

1 large Savoy cabbage, well-washed, trimmed and sliced
45 ml (3 tablespoons) double
cream
nutmeg to taste
salt and pepper

(serves 6)

Cook the cabbage in a little boiling salted water for 2 minutes, until just cooked and still crunchy. Drain well, and return to the saucepan. Stir in the cream, grated nutmeg and salt and pepper to taste. Serve at once.

RED CABBAGE AND ORANGE

900 g (2 lb) red cabbage, washed
4 oranges
150 ml (¼ pint) orange juice
50 g (2 oz) butter
salt and pepper
fresh parsley, chopped

(serves 8)

Slice the red cabbage finely. Peel the oranges and remove the pith. Slice the peel into thin, julienne strips, thinly slice and de-pip the flesh. Put a layer of cabbage in an ovenproof dish. On top of that, arrange some orange slices, strips of peel, and some orange juice. Dot some butter over this. Continue making layers in the same way, seasoning in between each layer. Cover with tin foil. Put in a pre-heated moderate oven (350°F, 180°C, gas 4) for an hour, or until tender. Before serving, fork through the cabbage, and add a little more butter, and a scattering of parsley.

LEMON CABBAGE

2 medium-sized green cabbages, washed and thinly sliced
juice of 2 lemons
50 g (2 oz) butter
pinch caraway seeds
salt and papper

(serves 8)

Place all the ingredients in a large pan, season with salt and pepper, and cook for 5 minutes – or until the cabbage has absorbed some of the flavourings, but is still crisp.

CAULIFLOWER WITH ALMONDS

2 medium cauliflowers, trimmed and washed
175 g (6 oz) white breadcrumbs
2 cloves garlic, very finely chopped
125 g (4 oz) almonds
125 g (4 oz) butter
salt and pepper

(serves 8)

Divide the cauliflower into florets and boil for 5 minutes, then drain and keep hot. Melt the butter, and fry the garlic until golden. Stir in the breadcrumbs and the almonds, and season well. Cook until golden brown and crisp. Serve the cauliflower with the breadcrumb mixture sprinkled on top.

COURCHEVEL COURGETTES

900 g (2 lbs) courgettes, washed and sliced

oil for deep frying

batter
225 g (8 oz) plain flour
1 egg
300 ml (½ pint) water or milk

30 ml (2 tablespoons) oil
salt and pepper

(serves 8)

Make the batter by mixing the milk or water with the flour. Season with salt. Add the egg, and beat until smooth. Mix in the oil, and leave aside to rest for 30 minutes. Dip the sliced courgettes into the batter, and deep fry in hot fat until golden brown. Drain on kitchen paper and season.

MAZOT SALAD

1 cucumber
3–4 cooked beetroots, skinned
2 small cartons natural yoghurt

45–60 ml (3–4 tablespoons) wine vinegar
salt and pepper

(serves 8)

Slice the cucumber finely (best done in a food processor). Arrange a layer around the outer edge of a large, flat serving dish. Slice the beetroot equally finely. Arrange a layer inside the cucumber ring, slightly overlapping. Continue, alternating the two vegetables until they are all used up. Season with salt and pepper. Mix the yoghurt and vinegar together well, and pour over the salad. Put in the fridge to chill before serving.

BL Chalet Girl kitchen planner tip
When clearing dishes between courses, scrape plates and put to soak in the sink, stack all cutlery in a saucepan to soak. It saves washing-up time.

NOODLES HAUTE NENDAZ

225 g (8 oz) cooked noodles
50 g (2 oz) mushrooms, cleaned and diced
125 g (4 oz) green pepper, de-seeded and diced
125 g (4 oz) red pepper, de-seeded and diced
400 g (14 oz) tin sweetcorn, drained
120 ml (8 tablespoons) vinaigrette (see p.104)
5 ml (1 teaspoon) mixed herbs
salt and pepper

(serves 8)

Mix all the ingredients together and serve.

RICE SALAD

225 g (8 oz) cooked long grain rice
120 ml (8 tablespoons) vinaigrette (see p.104)
125 g (4 oz) red pepper, de-seeded and diced
125 g (4 oz) green pepper, de-seeded and diced
400 g (14 oz) tin sweetcorn, drained
125 g (4 oz) packet salted peanuts
salt and pepper

(serves 8)

Mix all the ingredients together and season with salt and pepper. Serve in a glass bowl, sprinkled with chopped parsley.

SALAD ALDENTE

2 courgettes, washed and sliced
6 carrots, peeled and thinly sliced
½ cauliflower, cut into florets
300 ml (½ pint) mayonnaise
30 ml (2 tablespoons) sweet vinaigrette (see p.104)

(serves 6)

Mix the vinaigrette with the mayonnaise and toss with the prepared vegetables.

APPLE AND GRAPE SALAD WITH MINT DRESSING

4 apples, cored and sliced
3 sticks of celery, cleaned and chopped
450 g (1 lb) black grapes, halved
30 ml (2 tablespoons) mint, chopped

90 ml (6 tablespoons) vinaigrette (see below)
salt and pepper

(serves 8)

Toss all the ingredients together, season, and serve on a bed of lettuce leaves.

SWEET VINAIGRETTE

90 ml (6 tablespoons) olive oil
15 ml (1 tablespoon) French mustard

25 g (1 oz) sugar
30 ml (2 tablespoons) red wine vinegar

Combine all the ingredients, with salt and pepper to taste, in a jar. Put on the lid and shake very well.

VINAIGRETTE

90 ml (6 tablespoons) olive oil (sunflower if you prefer the taste)
10 ml (2 teaspoons) French mustard

30 ml (2 tablespoons) red wine vinegar
salt and pepper

Combine all the ingredients, with salt and pepper to taste, in a jar, Put on the lid and shake very well.

Chalet girl comment: This keeps well in the fridge.

PUDDINGS

To keep up their reputation of being 'the Fortnums of the ski business' the Bladon Lines Chalet Girls like to serve a variety of different and interesting puddings. Also, as the appetite of a guest who has been out skiing all day seems a bottomless pit, something substantial as well as delicious needs to be offered to make sure the customers are 'replete, content, well boozed and putting on weight while they stay with Bladon Lines', as the *Chalet Girl Manual* directs.

CHAMONIX CHEESECAKE

base
200 g (7 oz) digestive biscuits, crushed
15 ml (1 tablespoon) golden syrup
2.5 ml (½ teaspoon) ground cinnamon
50 g (2 oz) margarine

filling
175 g (6 oz) cream cheese
3 egg whites
1 lemon
200 ml (⅓ pint) double cream
75 g (3 oz) caster sugar
11.25 ml (2¼ teaspoons) powdered gelatine
a little water

(serves 6)

Grease a 17.5 cm (7 in) flan ring. Melt the margarine, syrup and cinnamon together in a pan. Mix in the crushed biscuits and press into the flan ring. Chill in the fridge until firm. Grate the lemon rind and squeeze the juice. Add the juice and water to the gelatine, and soak for 5 minutes. Then dissolve the gelatine over a pan of hot, but not boiling, water. Leave the mixture to cool. Cream the cheese, sugar and lemon rind together until smooth. Whip the cream until it holds its shape, and add to the cheese mixture. Stir in the gelatine. Whip the egg whites until stiff, and fold them into the mixture. Pour this into the flan ring, and leave to set for 2 hours. Decorate with rosettes of cream, and half slices of lemon dipped in sugar.

BANOFFI PIE

base
200 g (7 oz) digestive biscuits, crushed
50 g (2 oz) butter

filling
30 ml (2 tablespoons) caster sugar
5 ml (1 teaspoon) instant coffee powder
3 bananas, peeled
350 g (12 oz) tin sweetened condensed milk
300 ml (½ pint) double cream

(serves 6)

Cover the unopened tin of condensed milk with boiling water and simmer for 3 hours, keeping the tin submerged all the time, then allow to cool in the water. Meanwhile, melt the butter and stir in the biscuits to make the base. Press this mixture into a greased 17.5 cm (7 in) flan ring. Chill until set. Spread the cold, condensed milk (which will have turned into caramel) onto the base, and cover with slices of banana. Whip the cream, sugar and coffee together until thick. Spoon the mixture onto the biscuit base, and decorate with grated chocolate.

LE PERROQUET LEMON FREEZE

300 ml (½ pint) double cream
1 tin sweetened condensed milk
3 lemons
125 g (4 oz) cornflakes
125 g (4 oz) butter
30 ml (2 tablespoons) caster sugar

(serves 8)

Melt the butter and add the crushed cornflakes and sugar. Press this mixture into a base of a greased flan tin, and put in the fridge. Whip the cream until thick, and fold in the tin of condensed milk, plus the rind and juice of the lemons. Pour this over the base and leave to set in the freezer for about 2 hours. Take out 20 minutes before serving.

LEMON BISCUIT PUDDING

base
125 g (4 oz) digestive biscuits
50 g (2 oz) butter
25 g (1 oz) demerara sugar

topping
225 g (8 oz) cream cheese
150 ml (¼ pint) double cream
175 g (6 oz) can sweetened condensed milk
60 ml (4 tablespoons) lemon juice
grated rind of 1 lemon

(serves 6)

Make the base by crushing the biscuits, and mixing them with the melted butter and the demerara sugar. Press into a swiss roll tin and chill. Meanwhile, whip the cream, add the grated lemon rind and juice and the condensed milk. Pour this onto the biscuit base, and chill well before serving.

Chalet girls have to make the best of culinary disasters. One girl had oven failure in the middle of cooking profiteroles, and instead of rising up they flattened and spread dismally over the baking sheet. She split them anyway, forced in some cream, and covered the lot in butterscotch sauce. These 'Butterscotch Pats' were raved over in the way her profiteroles never were. Everyone wanted the recipe and begged her to cook them again. She just smiled enigmatically, said she *never* gave her recipes to anyone, and only prepared her special dishes once per party.

NO-CHEESE CHEESECAKE

175 g (6 oz) gingernuts
75 g (3 oz) butter
1 tin of condensed milk

2 large lemons
150 ml (¼ pint) double cream

(serves 8)

Crush the gingernuts and mix with the melted butter. Press this into a flan dish, and leave to cool. Mix the condensed milk with the whipped cream, and the grated rind of the lemons. Then slowly add as much of the juice of the lemons as you like, to taste. Pour into the base and put in the fridge for about 2 hours. Decorate with lemon slices or cream.

Chalet girl comment: Very good and quite tangy, depending on how much of the lemon juice you put in.

FROZEN CHOCOLATE CHEESECAKE

225 g (8 oz) digestive biscuits
75 g (3 oz) butter
225 g (8 oz) Philadelphia cheese
75 g (3 oz) chopped walnuts
175 g (6 oz) plain chocolate, melted

125 g (4 oz) caster sugar
2 beaten eggs
2 egg whites
5 ml (1 teaspoon) vanilla essence
150 ml (¼ pint) double cream

(serves 8)

Melt the butter. Crush the biscuits and mix with the butter. Press into a 20 cm (8 in) cake tin. Cream cheese with 50 g (2 oz) of the sugar and vanilla essence. Mix in the whole eggs, beaten, and the chocolate. Whisk cream and fold into this mixture. Whisk the egg whites and add the rest of the sugar. Fold this into the chocolate mixture. Add the nuts, and then pour the mixture on top of the biscuit base and freeze. Move into the fridge half an hour before serving.

Chalet girl comment: Really, really fattening, but scrummy!

MATTERHORN CHEESECAKE

filling
1 400 g (14 oz) tin pineapple rings

500 g (1 lb 2oz) Quark (or similar low-fat) cheese
2 beaten eggs

base
50 g (2 oz) butter
50 g (2 oz) sugar

200 g (7 oz) crushed digestive biscuits

topping
150 ml (¼ pint) soured cream or thick-set yoghurt

25 g (1 oz) icing sugar
vanilla essence to taste

(serves 8)

Make the base by adding the crushed biscuits to the melted butter with the sugar. Line a 20 cm (8 in) cake tin or flan dish with this mixture. Drain the pineapple. Keep one ring for decoration and purée the rest in the blender. Mix together the cheese and eggs and add the blended pineapple, then pour this over the biscuit base. Cook in a pre-heated moderate oven (350°F, 180°C, gas 4) for 1 hour. Leave to cool. Mix the topping ingredients together and smooth the mixture over the cheesecake. Put the reserved pineapple ring on top.

BL Chalet Girl tip
To make cream easier to whip, remove the carton from the fridge 1—2 hours beforehand.

TAQUINERIE CHEESECAKE

base
225 g (8 oz) digestive biscuits   125 g (4 oz) butter
filling
350 g (12 oz) cream cheese   400 g (14 oz) tin apricots
⅓ tin sweetened condensed milk   150 ml (¼ pint) double cream
juice of a lemon

(serves 8)

Crush the biscuits, melt the butter and mix the two together. Press into a 20 cm (8 in) loose-bottomed flan ring. Beat the cream cheese to soften it, and add the condensed milk and lemon juice. Pour this into the flan ring. Leave in the fridge for an hour to set. Pour most, but not all, the juice from the apricots away. Purée the apricots with the remaining liquid. Unmould the cheesecake and put on a serving plate. Whip the cream and pipe round the outside. Pour the apricot purée into the middle.

NIOBY FLAN

225 g (8 oz) petit beurre biscuits   1 lemon
75 g (3 oz) melted butter   500 g (1 lb) fromage blanc
125 g (4 oz) margarine   12–25 g (½–1 oz) gelatine
175 g (6 oz) caster sugar   soaked in peach juice
2 egg yolks   400 g (14 oz) tin peaches

(serves 8–10)

Crush the biscuits and mix with the melted butter and 50 g (2 oz) of the sugar. Flatten into a greased 36 cm (12 in) flan tin. Cream the margarine and the remainder of the caster sugar – 125 g (4 oz) – together. Beat in the egg yolks, fromage blanc and grated rind and juice of the lemon. Add the dissolved gelatine to the cheese mixture and pour onto the biscuit base. Put in the fridge to set. When it is firm, decorate the top with sliced tinned peaches.

GATEAU MONTAGNE

meringue
5 egg whites
150 g (5 oz) caster sugar

150 g (5 oz) icing sugar, sifted

filling
900 g (2 lbs) cooking apples, peeled, cored and sliced
1 lemon
150 g (5 oz) caster sugar
(serves 8)

50 g (2 oz) browned almond flakes
300 ml (½ pint) cream

Make the meringue mixture by beating the egg whites until stiff and then adding the two sugars. Beat until shiny. Make three large rounds with the mixture, the second slightly smaller than the first, the third smaller than that. Cook in a pre-heated, slow oven (300°F, 150°C, gas 2) for about 2 hours, until slightly golden and brittle. Make stewed apple by cooking with the sugar and lemon juice. Whip the cream. Make the gâteau by sandwiching the meringues with whipped cream and stewed apple, ending with a layer of stewed apple. Smooth some whipped cream around the edges to give it a solid effect, and spike the gateau with browned almonds.

Chalet girl comment: I concocted this recipe when the phone went as I was making a meringue basket. The mixture went floppy so I had to make flat meringues. But it is very impressive and almost foolproof.

The delicious lemon biscuit pud was chilling on the balcony when one of the guests went out for a breather. He scarcely noticed the strange squidging noise coming from his left foot, but the chalet girl noticed tell-tale signs of lemon fluff on the floor when he came back in. There was no time to make another pudding, so she whipped up lavish quantities of cream and forked it over the top to mask the footprint.

BANANA PUDDING A LA CHARLET

banana cake
125 g (4 oz) butter
2 beaten eggs
225 g (8 oz) plain flour
115 ml (7 tablespoons) milk
50 g (2 oz) chopped walnuts
350 g (12 oz) sugar

pinch salt
10 ml (2 teaspoons) baking powder
2.5 ml (½ teaspoon) vanilla essence
3 ripe bananas, mashed

meringue
250 g (9 oz) sugar

3 egg whites

topping
300 ml (½ pint) double cream
150 g (5 oz) raspberries or

strawberries
1 banana

(serves 12)

Cream the butter and sugar together, and add the eggs. Mix in the flour, salt and baking powder, and stir in the milk. Add the mashed bananas, walnuts and vanilla essence. Pour into a well-greased baking tin and cook in a moderate oven (350°F, 180°C, gas 4) for an hour. Leave to cool. Beat the egg whites until stiff. Fold in the sugar, and spoon onto a well-greased baking tray. Bake for 30 minutes in a pre-heated, slow oven (300°F, 150°C, gas 2). Turn the oven down to the lowest setting and cook for a further 30 minutes. Allow to cool. Crumble the banana cake into a large dish, crumble the meringue and mix it into the cake. Arrange the raspberries on top, pour over the cream, and add the sliced banana.

Chalet girl comment: I invented this when half the meringues for pudding caught fire so I had to improvise – and this was the delicious result.

STRAWBERRY PAVLOVA

4 egg whites
225 g (8 oz) caster sugar
10 ml (2 teaspoons) cold water
10 ml (2 teaspoons) wine vinegar
30 ml (2 tablespoons) cornflour

300 ml (½ pint) double cream
225 g (8 oz) strawberries, sliced
icing sugar
15 ml (1 tablespoon) chopped almonds

(serves 8)

Beat the egg whites and water until stiff. Sieve the cornflour and sugar into the beaten egg whites, and then gently fold them in. Finally, add the vinegar. Prepare a small baking sheet with greaseproof paper, slightly dampened with water. Pile on the mixture, spreading it lightly with a palette knife. Bake in a pre-heated, slow oven (325°F, 170°C, gas 3) for 45 minutes, or until light brown. Cool the meringue. Cover with whipped cream, and arrange the sliced strawberries on top. Sprinkle with sifted icing sugar and chopped nuts.

MERINGUE MERIBEL

600 ml (1 pint) whipping cream, lightly whipped to hold the meringue
brandy to taste
caster sugar to taste

2 medium-sized Pavlova cases, crumbled
450 g (1 lb) strawberries or raspberries

(serves 8)

Mix everything gently together, except for the fruit, adding as much brandy as you dare. Put the mixture in a nice dish in the freezer for about 2 hours. Remove 10 minutes before serving, and arrange the fruit on top.

Chalet girl comment: It is *very* rich!

MERINGUE ICE CREAM

2 medium-sized Pavlova cases, or a 4-egg quantity of meringue
½ litre (18 fl oz) whipped cream
½ litre (18 fl oz) vanilla ice cream

50 g (2 oz) sultanas
50 g (2 oz) glacé cherries
50 g (2 oz) dried fruits
60 ml (4 tablespoons) kirsch/ brandy or other liqueur
200 g (7 oz) frozen raspberries

(serves 6)

Whip the cream until really thick, adding the alcohol in the last few seconds. Add the ice cream and stir into the cream. Break up the meringue and add with the dried fruit and cherries. Mix well, and pour into serving dishes. Place the dishes in the freezer until the mixture becomes solid. Defrost the raspberries and purée them – you can sieve out the pips if you prefer. Serve the ice cream unmoulded with the raspberries as sauce over the top.

Chalet girl comment: This is an excellent way of using up meringues that have gone wrong. When preparing this in a chalet I would put it outside in the snow to freeze.

It never matters to a chalet girl if she finds that the fridge in her chalet is on the small side. The area surrounding the chalet is one vast fridge, guaranteed to remain cold even during a power cut. The window sill, of course, is the top favourite cold shelf, and consequently sometimes the site of culinary disasters. One girl was busy preparing three courses at once, and put the uncooked meringue mixture for her Pavlova on its baking sheet on the window sill, and then forgot about it. When she turned round to put it in the oven, she saw to her horror the very last bit slithering off the baking sheet and out of the window. As she looked out, appalled, there was no discernable sight of the frothy white mixture, which had perfectly blended with the clean white snow. There was nothing to do but make another batch quickly.

TARTE AUX ABRICOTS

pastry
100 g (4 oz) flour
25 g (1 oz) caster sugar

50 g (2 oz) butter
2 egg yolks

crème patissière
2 egg yolks
25 g (1 oz) flour
vanilla essence to taste

50 g (2 oz) caster sugar
250 ml (8 fl oz) milk
25 g (1 oz) butter

glaze
45 ml (3 tablespoons) apricot jam

2 tins apricot halves
50 g (2 oz) toasted almonds

(serves 6)

Make up the pastry by sifting the flour with a pinch of salt onto a working surface. Make a well in the centre and add the sugar, butter and egg yolks. Mix well together, bringing in the flour from the edge. Knead lightly until smooth. Wrap in foil and chill for 15 minutes. Make the crème patissière by blending the egg yolks and sugar together and whisking until thick and creamy. Add the flour and 15 ml (1 tablespoon) of the milk, and whisk well. Line a flan tin with the pastry, cover and chill for another 15 minutes. Cook the pastry case for 15 minutes in a pre-heated hot oven (450°F, 230°C, gas 8). Bring the remaining milk to the boil and pour onto the egg mixture. Heat in a clean pan to a simmer, stirring all the time. Add the butter and vanilla essence to taste. Cool, and pour into the flan base. Arrange the apricots cut side down on top, the almonds in between. Boil the jam for a few minutes, sieve, and use to glaze the top of the flan. Chill and serve.

Chalet girl comment: This is good with strawberries too. Don't make it too long before serving or the pastry will go soggy.

CHOCOLATE HONEY PROFITEROLES

choux pastry
4 beaten eggs
125 g (4 oz) butter or margarine

300 ml (½ pint) cold water
150 g (5 oz) flour
pinch salt

filling
150 ml (¼ pint) double cream
125 g (4 oz) plain cooking chocolate

30 ml (2 tablespoons) honey
30 ml (2 tablespoons) water
50 g (2 oz) butter

(serves 6)

To make the choux pastry, bring the water and fat to the boil, and remove from heat. Add the sieved flour and salt, and mix with a wooden spoon. Return to a moderate heat and stir continuously until the mixture leaves the side of the pan. Remove from the heat and allow to cool. Gradually add the beaten eggs, mixing well. The paste should be a dropping consistency. Put the mixture into a large piping bag, using a 1.25 cm (½ in) plain tube. Pipe the pastry onto a greased baking sheet into pieces the size of a walnut. Bake in a pre-heated, moderately hot oven (425°F, 220°C, gas 7) for approximately 30 minutes. Leave to cool. Split with a knife. Fill each profiterole with the cream (whipped until it holds its shape) and pile onto a plate. Melt the chocolate, honey, water and butter together, and pour over the profiteroles.

TOFFEE TREAT

2 tins sweetened condensed milk
6 bananas

300 ml (½ pint) double cream, whipped
450 g (1 lb) puff pastry

(serves 8)

Simmer the unopened tins of milk in boiling water for 4 hours – until it has turned into toffee. Leave to cool completely. Meanwhile, roll out the puff pastry and cut into two circles. Brush with a little milk, and dust with caster sugar. Cook in a pre-heated moderately hot oven (350°–400°F, 180°–200°C, gas 4–6) for 30 minutes. Leave to cool. Place the toffee on one layer, and cover with chopped bananas and whipped cream. Place the other round of pastry on top.

ZERMATT APPLE TARTS

450 g (1 lb) packet frozen puff pastry
1 large or 2 small cooking apples

30 ml (2 tablespoons) apricot jam
lemon juice

(serves 6)

Roll out the pastry to 0.4 cm (⅙ in) thick. Using a teacup, cut rounds of about 8 cm (3½ in) diameter. Slice apples thinly and arrange sections neatly on the pastry. Squeeze a little lemon juice over the tarts. Glaze each tart with about 5 ml (1 teaspoon) hot apricot jam each. Cook in a pre-heated hot oven (450°F, 230°C, gas 8) for 10 minutes, or until the pastry is fully risen and golden brown. Serve at once with vanilla ice-cream or cream – or, better still, both!

Chalet girl comment: This can be prepared in advance, but cooked at the last minute.

NOSTALGIA PUDDING

100 g (3½ oz) butter
90 ml (6 tablespoons) marmalade
30 ml (2 tablespoons) lemon juice
150 g (5 oz) breadcrumbs

25 g (1 oz) self-raising flour
75 g (3 oz) caster sugar
3 eggs
2.5 ml (½ teaspoon) bicarbonate of soda
50 g (2 oz) plain chocolate chips

(serves 8)

Butter a 1.1–1.4 litre (1¾–2¼ pint) pudding basin. Melt the marmalade and butter together and stir in the lemon juice. Put the breadcrumbs in a mixing bowl, and add the flour and caster sugar. Stir in the melted jam and butter. Whisk eggs until pale and frothy and stir them thoroughly into the mixture with the bicarbonate of soda. Finally, stir in the chocolate pieces. Pour into the pudding basin and cover with a piece of foil, pleated in the middle to allow the pudding to rise. Steam for 2–2¼ hours.

A Christmas pudding in a red plastic dish was put on to boil. The pan boiled dry and the red plastic melted all over the pudding and then caught fire. The plucky chalet girl ran outside with it and launched it sizzling into a snowdrift and then poured a bucket of water over it, while the guests stood by laughing and taking pictures. When it was cooled, the chalet girl peeled off the plastic to inspect the damage. The pudding inside was unharmed, so she put it back into the oven to cook. It was served up flaming (once again) with brandy, and then covered in cream. The guests all said it was the best they'd ever had.

SWISS APPLE TART

pastry
300 g (10 oz) plain flour   150 g (5 oz) butter
25 g (1 oz) caster sugar

crème patissière
2 egg yolks   50 g (2 oz) caster sugar
25 g (1 oz) plain flour   250 ml (8 fl oz) milk
vanilla essence to taste   25 g (1 oz) butter

filling
6 eating apples   jam
5 ml (1 teaspoon) ground   sugar to taste
   cinnamon   nutmeg to taste
30 ml (2 tablespoons) apricot   30 ml (2 tablespoons) water

(serves 8–10)

Rub fat into the sifted flour, with a pinch of salt. Add the sugar and mix together, binding with water. Roll out, and line a 30 cm (12 in) flan tin. Prick the pastry. Make up crème patissière by blending egg yolks and sugar together and whisking until thick and creamy. Add flour, milk and vanilla essence, whisking well as you bring it to a simmer. Cook for 5 minutes. Beat in the butter. Cool, and pour onto the pastry. Peel, core and finely slice the apples. Starting at the outer edge of the flan, make a circle of overlapping slices, then another circle within this, continuing until all the apple is used up, and the crème patissière covered. Sprinkle with sugar, cinnamon and nutmeg. Bake in a pre-heated, moderate oven (350°F, 180°C, gas 4) until the apples are golden and the pastry is cooked. Bring the jam to boil with the water, and brush it over the apples and pastry. Serve cold, with whipped cream.

BL Chalet Girl kitchen planner tip
Keep a large jar suitable for vegetable left-overs for soup.

CHOCOLATE ROULADE

6 eggs, separated
225 g (8 oz) caster sugar
1.25 ml (¼ teaspoon) vanilla essence
50 g (2 oz) cocoa powder

150 ml (¼ pint) whipped cream
1 small orange, peeled and cut into thin rounds
sifted icing sugar

(serves 6)

Whisk the egg yolks with the vanilla essence and sugar, until creamy. Sieve and fold in the cocoa powder. Whisk egg whites until stiff but not brittle, and fold into the egg yolk mixture. Line a tin 30 cm x 20 cm (12 in x 8 in) with greaseproof paper, and pour in the mixture. Bake in a pre-heated moderate oven (375°F, 190°C, gas 5) for 20 minutes. Turn out onto a damp teatowel, strip off the paper and cool. Cover with half the whipped cream, and use the towel to help you roll it up. Place the roulade on a serving dish and decorate with icing sugar. Pipe rosettes of the remaining whipped cream on top, and place a slice of orange between each rosette.

BISCUIT TORTINI

300 ml (½ pint) double cream
2 egg whites
pinch salt
60 ml (4 tablespoons) caster sugar

125 g (4 oz) blanched almonds, coarsely chopped
60 ml (4 tablespoons) brandy or marsala
sliced toasted almonds

(serves 6)

Chill a 1 kilo (2 lb) loaf tin. Place the egg whites in a large, clean, dry mixing bowl and add the salt. Whisk until it forms peaks. Whisk in the sugar, 15 ml (1 tablespoon) at a time. When all the sugar has been added, whisk until sleek and glossy. Whisk cream until it holds its shape. Fold the cream into the meringue mixture, together with the almonds. Add the marsala, and pile into the chilled loaf tin. Freeze for 3–4 hours. Dip the container in hot water, turn out, and sprinkle with sliced browned almonds.

HAZELNUT GALETTE

175 g (6 oz) butter or margarine
60 g (2½ oz) caster sugar
140 g (4½ oz) plain flour
75 g (3 oz) hazelnuts, ground (or 6 whole hazelnuts)
675 g (1½ lbs) dessert apples, peeled, cored and sliced
3 cloves
grated rind and juice of 1 lemon
15 ml (1 tablespoon) apricot jam
50 g (2 oz) sultanas
150 ml (¼ pint) double cream
45 ml (3 tablespoons) icing sugar, sifted

(serves 6)

Beat the butter or margarine with the caster sugar until light and fluffy. Add the flour and ground nuts, and knead until smooth. Chill for 1 hour. Cook the apples, jam, cloves, lemon juice and rind together until the apples slices are tender, but still whole. Roll the pastry into three rounds. Cook in a moderate oven (350°F, 180°C, gas 4) for 20 minutes. Allow to cool slightly. Divide one round into 6 segments. Whip the cream. Remove the cloves from the apple mixture. Put half the apples and a layer of whipped cream on one of the pastry rounds. Place the other pastry round on top. Put the rest of the apples, and most of the cream on top. Arrange the 6 pastry segments on top of this. Decorate each segment with a rosette of whipped cream and a hazelnut. Sprinkle with icing sugar.

BANANA ICE CREAM

600 ml (1 pint) double cream
4 large bananas, peeled
225 g (8 oz) caster sugar
juice of 4 oranges
juice of 4 lemons

(serves 8)

Cream the bananas and sugar together until smooth. Whip the cream until it holds its shape and fold into the banana mixture with the juices. Freeze for 24 hours. Serve garnished with sliced bananas.

FRUIT SALAD ST MORITZ

225 g (8 oz) black cherries
1 watermelon
2 peaches
2 oranges
1 small box strawberries, hulled
2 bananas, peeled

225 g (8 oz) black grapes
2 red apples, cored
125 g (4 oz) sugar
100 ml (4 fl oz) water
30 ml (2 tablespoons) kirsch
 liqueur

(serves 6)

Peel and segment the orange. Remove the pith and cut the rind into thin strips, and put in a pan with the sugar and water, and heat to form a syrup. Leave to cool, and add the kirsch. Stone and slice the cherries, peaches and grapes. Slice the top off the watermelon. Using a knife, cut the edge carefully to produce a zig-zag effect. Scoop out the melon with a metal spoon and cut the chunks into squares. Finely slice the banana, apples and strawberries. Mix all the fruit with kirsch syrup, and spoon it all back into the watermelon case. Chill before serving.

BL Chalet Girl economy tip
Use margarine as much as possible, especially where the taste doesn't 'show' – it's cheaper – and better for you if it is 'high in polyunsaturates'.

COFFEE AND KAHLUA SYLLABUB

600 ml (1 pint) double cream
2 liqueur glasses Kahlua or Tia Maria
125 g (4 oz) caster sugar

10 ml (2 teaspoons) instant coffee powder
grated chocolate

(serves 8)

Whip the above ingredients together until quite thick. Pour into wine glasses or glass dishes, then chill. Serve decorated with grated chocolate.

DARK AND WHITE CHOCOLATE PARFAIT

300 g (10 oz) dark chocolate
300 g (10 oz) white chocolate
300 ml (½ pint) double cream

125 ml (5 fl oz) milk
2 eggs
50 g (2 oz) caster sugar

sauce
300 g (10 oz) raspberries

75 g (3 oz) icing sugar

(serves 10–15)

Melt the chocolates in separate bowls over hot water. Whisk the eggs and sugar together, until they form a 'ribbon', that is, the mixture is thick and creamy. Heat the cream and milk together gently, until they are blood temperature. Using a whisk, slowly add half the cream mixture to the dark chocolate, then fold in half the egg mixture. Do the same with the white chocolate, and leave both mixtures to cool thoroughly. Line a rectangular mould with clingfilm. Using a ladle, cover the bottom of the mould with dark chocolate, followed by a layer of white. Try to make three thin layers of each colour. Put in the freezer for 24 hours. Serve with the sauce, made by puréeing the raspberries with the sugar.

Chalet girl comment: This dish is superb if you like chocolate. When it is served the two chocolate colours give a marbled effect.

One Christmas the reps bought a job-lot of frozen turkeys for all the chalets in their resort. They delivered them to the chalets some days before Christmas, so they had to be kept frozen until needed. One chalet, without a deep-freeze, decided to bury the turkey deep in the snow outside to keep it frozen.

On Christmas Eve they went to retrieve it. To their horror they found tiny footprints leading up to the mound in the snow and more little footprints leading away from it on the other side. On top was a little yellow patch.

The turkey tasted fine on the day.

CHOCCY BICCY PUD

125 g (4 oz) butter
175 g (6 oz) block chocolate, or chocolate dots
30 ml (2 tablespoons) drinking chocolate powder
225 g (8 oz) digestive biscuits
15 ml (1 tablespoon) golden syrup

(serves 6)

Melt the butter in a pan with the syrup and chocolate powder. At the same time, melt the block chocolate in a bowl over hot water. Crush the biscuits and add them to the butter mixture, then press into a greased swiss roll tin. Cover with melted chocolate, and mark into sections. Chill. Serve decorated with cream.

Chalet girl comment: This is also good with the addition of brandy-soaked sultanas.

YOGHURT PUDDING

½ small carton of plain yoghurt per person
50 g (2 oz) nuts per person (walnuts, almonds, brazils, hazelnuts)
1 piece of fruit per person – fresh, chopped or the equivalent tinned
5 ml (1 teaspoon) molasses per person
15 ml (1 tablespoon) double cream per person
25 g (1 oz) raisins per person

Mix all the ingredients together, chill and serve.

MARS BAR SAUCE FOR VANILLA ICE CREAM

4 Mars bars
a little water
a slosh of brandy, Grand Marnier, or similar

(serves 6)

Break or slice the Mars bar into very small pieces. Melt these in a thick saucepan over a very low heat, adding just enough water to make it runny. Add the liqueur. This is best done just before serving. If you make it earlier, it will need reheating again – over a very low heat, stirring constantly. Pour the sauce over slices of vanilla ice cream.

RICH CHOCOLATE GATEAU

225 g (8 oz) chocolate chips
125 g (4 oz) unsalted butter

45 ml (3 tablespoons) icing sugar, sifted
3 no. 3 eggs, separated

(serves 6)

Melt the chocolate chips in a bowl over hot water. When runny, whisk, gradually adding flakes of the butter. When all the butter is incorporated, add the sugar, and finally the egg yolks. Whip the whites until stiff, and then combine with the chocolate mixture. Pour into a tin and chill.

Chalet girl comment: This keeps for weeks, and freezes well.

YOGHURT APPLE BRULEE

450 g (1 lb) cooking apples
25 g (1 oz) butter
topping
150 ml (¼ pint) double cream
150 ml (¼ pint) yoghurt

demerara sugar to taste

75 g (3 oz) demerara sugar

(serves 6)

Peel, core and slice the apples, and cook them slowly in the butter. When they are cooked, beat to a purée, and add demerara sugar sparingly, so as not to make it too sweet. Divide this mixture between 6 ramekins. Lightly whip the cream, and combine it with the yoghurt. Spoon this over the apple purée and smooth the tops. Chill. Sprinkle the demerara sugar evenly over each pudding, and glaze quickly under a hot grill. Chill for a further 2 hours before serving.

LEMON CAN'T-LEAVE-ME-ALONE PUDDING

3 eggs
1 lemon jelly
juice of 1 lemon

75 g (3 oz) caster sugar
1 small jar lemon curd
150 ml (¼ pint) whipped cream

(serves 6)

Melt jelly in 300 ml (½ pint) boiling water. Add 150 ml (¼ pint) cold water and the lemon juice. Separate eggs, and beat the whites until stiff. Beat the yolks and sugar into the jelly mixture, and then fold this into the egg whites. Leave to set overnight. When set, spread the lemon curd over the top, and cover with whipped cream.

MELON IN LIME

1 cantaloupe melon
1 honeydew melon
1 small watermelon
225 g (8 oz) redcurrants (or the equivalent tinned)

juice of 1 lime (or bottled, unsweetened lime juice, or lemon juice)
grated rind of ½ lime, or lemon

(serves 6)

Cut the melons in half, removing the seeds. Scoop out the insides, using a melon scoop if possible, or cut out and chop into bite-sized pieces. Mix with the redcurrants, then mix the rind with juice and pour over the fruit. Pile back into the melon halves, and decorate with sprigs of fresh mint.

Chalet girl comment: This is a very tasty and refreshing pudding. It must be eaten chilled and fresh.

CITRUS SURPRISE

3 egg whites
150 ml (¼ pint) whipping cream
15 g (½ oz) gelatine
450 ml (¾ pint) lemon yoghurt

450 ml (¾ pint) plain yoghurt
450 ml (¾ pint) cherry yoghurt
2 bananas

(serves 8)

Whip the cream. Dissolve the gelatine according to directions. Whip the egg whites, and fold in the whipped cream and the mixed yoghurts. Mash the bananas with the cooled gelatine, and fold this into the yoghurt mixture. Pour into serving dishes and leave for about an hour in the fridge to set.

CHOCOLATE WILLIES

1 banana per person
50 g (2 oz) chocolate per person
15 ml (1 tablespoon) milk per person
alcohol to taste (brandy, whisky, Cointreau)

Melt the chocolate with the milk, adding extra milk if necessary so that the mixture is not too rich and thick. Add the alcohol to taste. Pour the mixture over the bananas and bake in a pre-heated moderate oven (350°F, 180°C, gas 4) for 15–20 minutes. Serve hot.

Chalet girl comment: It gets a laugh – and tastes good.

SNOW-CAPPED MOUNTAINS

225 g (8 oz) plain chocolate
6 egg yolks
12 egg whites
90 ml (6 tablespoons) cherry brandy
150 ml (¼ pint) double cream
grated chocolate

(serves 8)

Melt the chocolate. Remove from heat. Add the egg yolks, and stir rapidly. Whisk the egg whites until stiff, and fold in the chocolate and brandy – quickly as it sets hard. Pour into a serving dish, and leave to set in the fridge. Beat the cream until stiff, and cover the chocolate with it, forming it into peaks with a fork. Sprinkle with grated chocolate to decorate.

Chalet girl comment: It is very quick to make and so delicious that everyone always asks for the recipe. It is similar to chocolate mousse, but denser.

NORWEGIAN CREAM

600 ml (1 pint) milk
4 eggs
50 g (2 oz) sugar
4 drops vanilla essence
120 ml (8 tablespoons) apricot jam, melted

125 g (4 oz) plain chocolate, grated
300 ml (½ pint) whipping cream

(serves 8)

Divide the melted jam between 8 ramekins. Warm the milk, and beat in the eggs, sugar and vanilla essence. Strain, and pour over the jam in the ramekins. Place the ramekins in a roasting tin, and pour around enough water to come half-way up the sides. Cook in a pre-heated moderate oven (325°F, 160°C, gas 3) for about 30 minutes, until set. Leave to cool. Whip up the cream, and pile on top of the custard. Decorate with the grated chocolate.

APRICOT AMBROSIA

2 × 400 g (14½ oz) tins apricot halves
30 ml (2 tablespoons) clear honey

125 g (4 oz) ratafia biscuits
300 ml (½ pint) whipped cream
30 ml (2 tablespoons) flaked, toasted almonds

(serves 8)

Drain the apricots, and blend with the honey until smooth. Break the ratafias into bite-sized pieces, if they are not already small. Fold into the whipped cream with the apricot purée. Sprinkle with the almonds, and serve immediately.

Every chalet girl knows the difficult customer – often in a group of otherwise perfectly charming guests. There was one guest who complained about everything. If he was given a Mars bar in his packed lunch, he would say he was entitled to two – *that* sort. One night he was kicking up a fuss about the walnut and apricot crumble. There was nothing about it he liked, and his moans were spoiling the evening. For once, this insensitive creature seemed to notice a drop in the temperature of the atmosphere, so he tried to make a joke of it by saying he would have the crumble in his sandwich for his packed lunch. Lo and behold, when he unwrapped his roll the next day he found that his command had been obeyed. The customer is always right.

BRANDY AND GINGER CREAM

600 ml (1 pint) natural yoghurt
300 ml (½ pint) double cream
2 × 400 g (14 oz) tins raspberries or stone black cherries

2 x 225 g (8 oz) packets ginger biscuits
1 wine glass brandy

(serves 8)

Break the biscuits roughly into pieces and soak in the brandy. Meanwhile, whip the cream until thick but not stiff and fold into the yoghurt. Drain the fruit and add to the cream mixture with the biscuits. Add some of the juice from the fruit to taste, and more brandy if desired. Serve within 2 hours.

Chalet girl comment: Brandy snaps go well with this.

VERY EASY LEMON ICE CREAM

grated rind of 2 lemons
juice of 3 lemons
175 g (6 oz) caster sugar

300 ml (½ pint) milk
300 ml (½ pint) double cream

(serves 6)

Beat the rind, juice and sugar together until smooth and frothy on top. Add the cream slowly, and then the milk, beating all the time until it is very well mixed. Pour into a bowl and freeze. You can take out after 4 hours and beat it again, but it is not strictly necessary. Remove from the freezer just before serving as it melts very quickly. Turn out onto a plate and decorate with slices of lemon and serve with biscuits.

ORANGES IN CARAMEL

16 large oranges
800 g (1 lb 12 oz) granulated sugar

300 ml (½ pint) cold water
300 ml (½ pint) warm water

(serves 8)

Cut rind off the oranges, and then remove the pith. Slice the oranges, removing any pips. Make julienne strips from the rind of half the oranges, and blanch for a minute in boiling water. To make the caramel, put the sugar and cold water together in a pan. When the sugar has dissolved, bring to the boil. *But don't stir.* The caramel will change colour quickly, so keep a close watch. Remove it from the heat as soon as it turns light brown. Cover your arm with a cloth, and then quickly and carefully pour the caramel into the warm water. Put back on the heat and dissolve again. Allow to cool, and pour onto the orange slices. Scatter the julienne strips over the top, and decorate with whipped cream.

Chalet girl comment: This is nicest when served thoroughly chilled. Almond or ginger biscuits go well with it, as it is not very filling on its own.

BL Chalet Girl garnish
A swirl of cream in the shape of a heart gets even the most unromantic people smiling.

CREME CLARMONT

600 g (1 lb 5 oz) Ricotta or fromage frais cheese
480 ml (¾ pint) cream

400 g (14 oz) tin pineapple
4 bananas
50 g (2 oz) demerara sugar

(serves 8)

Purée the bananas with the contents of the pineapple tin. Beat the cheese and cream together until thick. Stir in the puréed fruit. Pour into 8 ramekins, or one large serving dish. Sprinkle with the demerara sugar just before serving. Kirsch or other liqueur may be added, if desired, to the purée.

KLOSTERS CHOCOLATE KRUNCH

125 g (4 oz) margarine or butter
125 g (4 oz) sieved icing sugar
60 ml (4 tablespoons) golden syrup
60 ml (4 tablespoons) cocoa

175 g (6 oz) cornflakes
2 tins mandarin oranges, drained (or fresh fruit)
300 ml (½ pint) cream

(serves 8)

Melt the margarine, add the sugar, syrup and cocoa, take off the heat and add the cornflakes. Divide the mixture between two greased 20 cm (8 in) cake tins, preferably with removable bases. Allow to cool in the fridge until set. Just before serving, remove from the tins and decorate each cake with whipped cream, and the fruit arranged on top.

Chalet girl comment: This looks very attractive decorated with alternating slices of banana and kiwi fruit.

CHARLOTTE AUX FRAMBOISES ET FROMAGE BLANC

500 g (1 lb) boudoir sponge fingers
syrup made with 125 g (4 oz) sugar to 300 ml (½ pint) water
dash of liqueur
500 g (1 lb) pot fromage blanc

60 ml (4 tablespoons) double cream
30 ml (2 tablespoons) caster sugar
750 g (1 lb 10 oz) raspberries

(serves 8)

Add some liqueur to the sugar syrup. Mix the fromage blanc with the cream and sugar. Dip the biscuits into the sugar syrup, and use to line the sides and base of a charlotte mould. Fill with alternate layers of raspberries and fromage blanc mixture, and when these are all used up, put a lid of syrup-soaked biscuits on the top. Press a plate down onto this and leave in the fridge for 12 hours. Turn out onto another plate, and serve.

CAKES

'Bake a Fresh Cake Every Day' is an instruction engraved on every Bladon Lines Chalet Girl's heart. Something different in the form of cakes or biscuits must be provided every single day of the guests' holiday. Anything left over must be used up in cooking, not served the next day. Girls who pride themselves on their baking find that the high altitude in the Alps plays havoc with their favourite recipes. Which means that all the cakes and biscuits here are pretty foolproof under any conditions.

BANANA BREAD

285 g (9 oz) butter
285 g (9 oz) caster sugar
565 g (1 lb 3 oz) plain flour
4 eggs
10 ml (2 teaspoons) bicarbonate soda
4 very ripe bananas, mashed
20–30 ml (4–6 teaspoons) sour milk

(serves 8)

Cream the butter and sugar. Add the eggs, flour and all other ingredients. Place in a greased, 1 kilo (2 lb) loaf tin. Bake in a pre-heated moderate oven (350°F, 180°C, gas 4) for an hour, until a needle pushed into it comes out clean.

Chalet girl comment: This is the simplest thing to make for tea time, and totally foolproof – especially in the Alps where cakes can often flop. As a change, you can add a few walnuts.

APPLE SCONES

450 g (1 lb) self-raising flour
pinch of salt
125 g (4 oz) butter or firm margarine
50 g (2 oz) caster sugar
50 g (2 oz) soft brown sugar
300 ml (½ pint) milk
1 apple, peeled, cored and diced

(serves 8)

Sieve flour and salt in a bowl. Rub in the fat and add the caster sugar, apple and milk. Mix to a soft, but not sticky, dough with a knife. Turn out onto a lightly floured board. Cut into 5 cm (2 inch) rounds, about 1 cm (½ inch) thick. Place on a greased baking sheet, brush with a little extra milk and sprinkle with brown sugar. Bake in a pre-heated hot oven (450°F, 230°C, gas 8) for 10 minutes until well-risen and brown.

CHOCOLATE RIPPLE CAKE

225 g (8 oz) packet of digestive biscuits
1 jar of jam
300 ml (½ pint) whipping cream
300 ml (½ pint) sweet white wine or sherry
2 x 125 g (4 oz) packets cooking chocolate dots
chocolate flake or jar of smarties to decorate

(serves 8)

Dip a biscuit in the wine or sherry and spread jam on one side. Do the same with another biscuit, and sandwich them together, standing them upright on a plate. Continue until you use up all the biscuits – you should have a slim log-shape on your plate. Melt the chocolate, and pour it over the cake, then put it in the fridge to set. Beat the cream and spread it over the chocolate. Decorate with the crumbled chocolate flake or smarties. Slice the cake diagonally, or it will fall apart.

YOGHURT CAKE

1 small carton yoghurt (strawberry, apricot, or any flavour)

using yoghurt container as a measure:

1 measure caster sugar
1 measure sunflower oil
3 measures plain flour
10 ml (2 teaspoons) baking powder
4 eggs
45 ml (3 tablespoons) jam, the same flavour as the yoghurt
sifted icing sugar

(serves 10–14)

Mix all ingredients except the jam well together, either by hand or using a food processor. Place into a greased 20 cm (8 in) cake tin and bake in the centre of a moderate oven (350°F, 180°C, gas 4) for 40–50 minutes. When cool, cut in half and spread one half with the jam, and some extra yoghurt, if you like. Put the other half on top and sprinkle with icing sugar.

Chalet girl comment: The baking powder measurement is for girls cooking in the Alps. Elsewhere you can use self-raising flour and no baking powder.

ENERGY CAKE

250 g (9 oz) muesli
50 g (2 oz) sultanas
50 g (2 oz) glacé cherries

400 g (14 oz) chocolate dots
250 g (9 oz) margarine
60 ml (4 tablespoons) treacle

(serves 10)

Melt 200 g (7 oz) of the margarine with the treacle. Add the muesli and dried fruit. Tip into a flan ring and flatten onto the bottom. Bake in a pre-heated moderate oven (350°F, 180°C, gas 4) for 10 minutes. Cool. Melt the chocolate with the remaining 50 g (2 oz) margarine. Pour this over the cooled muesli mixture. Leave in the fridge for 1 hour.

APRICOT CRUMBLE PARTY SLICE

base
2 kg (4 lbs 4 oz) plain flour
¾ kg (1 lb 10 oz) margarine
¾ kg (1 lb 10 oz) butter

½ kg (1 lb 1oz) sugar
palmful salt

filling
⅓ large tin apricot jam

5 ml (1 teaspoon) ginger

topping
1 kg (2 lbs 2 oz) plain flour
½ kg (1 lb 1 oz) butter

¼ kg (8 oz) sugar

(serves 100 – for smaller numbers, alter measurements accordingly!)

Make the base by melting the butter and margarine together. Beat in the sugar, then gradually add the flour and the palmful of salt. Press into two ready-greased large baking trays. Cover the base with an even layer of apricot jam, and sieve the ginger over the top. Prepare the topping by rubbing the butter into the sugar and flour to make a crumble. Layer this evenly over the jam. Bake in a pre-heated moderate oven (350°F, 180°C, gas 4) for about 1½ hours until golden. Mark into 100 portions and allow to cool in the tin.

Chalet girl comment: This is served in a chalet hotel where there are sixty or seventy hungry guests, but is perfect for a party.

STRAWBERRY CAKE

175 g (6 oz) *butter or margarine*
175 g (6 oz) *caster sugar*
3 *eggs*
5 ml (1 teaspoon) *lemon juice*
225 g (8 oz) *plain flour*
5 ml (1 teaspoon) *baking powder*
45 ml (3 tablespoons) *milk*
350 g (12 oz) *strawberry jam*
sifted icing sugar

(serves 8–12)

Grease and flour a 20 cm (8 in) cake tin. Cream the fat and sugar together. Beat in the eggs, one at a time. Add the lemon juice and stir in the flour, baking powder and milk. Mix in the jam. Pour this mixture into the tin and bake in the middle of a pre-heated moderate oven (350°F, 180°C, gas 4) for 1½ hours. Turn onto a rack and cool. Sprinkle with icing sugar before serving.

Chalet girl comment: Another foolproof cake that even survives the dodgy baking conditions in the Alps.

ORANGE SYRUP CAKE

175 g (6 oz) *self-raising flour*
pinch of salt
125 g (4 oz) *caster sugar*
finely grated rind and juice of 1 large orange
2 *large eggs*
15–30 ml (1–2 tablespoons) *milk*
125 g (4 oz) *butter*
125 g (4 oz) *icing sugar*
sifted icing sugar to decorate

(serves 6–8)

Sift the flour and salt. Cream the butter, sugar and orange rind until soft and light. Lightly mix the eggs, and beat into the mixture a little at a time, adding a little flour to help the two mix, if necessary. Fold in the remaining flour and a little milk to make a soft dropping consistency. Spoon the mixture into a greased and lined shallow 20 cm (8 in) sponge tin, and spread it level. Bake in the centre of a pre-heated moderate oven (350°F, 180°C, gas 4) for about 30 minutes until risen and lightly brown. Meanwhile, strain the orange juice and put it into a saucepan with the icing sugar. Heat gently so that the sugar dissolves. Prick the hot cake all over with a fine skewer and spoon the hot syrup over it. The cake will soak it up eventually. Leave until quite cold. Loosen the sides of the cake and remove from the tin. Dust generously with icing sugar and serve.

AUSTRIAN LINZERTORTE

500 g (1 lb) flour
5 ml (1 teaspoon) baking
  powder
250 g (8 oz) butter
250 g (8 oz) sugar

2 eggs
grated rind of 1 lemon
60–90 ml (4–6 tablespoons)
  redcurrant jelly
whipped cream

(serves 8–10)

Sieve the flour and make a hole in the centre. Sprinkle the baking powder round the edge. Chop the butter and add to the middle, followed by the sugar and grated lemon rind. Make another hole in the centre of this and break the eggs into it. Then, drawing the flour in from the outer edges, combine the ingredients to form a ball of dough. Line a baking tray with foil and oil well. Use half the mixture to cover the bottom of the tin, then spread a layer of redcurrant jelly over it. Roll the other half of the pastry out and cut into strips and lay them over the jam, making a lattice pattern. Bake in a pre-heated moderately hot oven (400°F, 200°C, gas 6) for 25 minutes. When cool, cut into slices and serve – in Tyrolean tradition – with whipped cream.

Chalet girl comment: I was shown how to make this cake in Germany when I answered 'Ja' to a question I thought meant 'Did you like it?' I was promptly taken into the kitchen for a demonstration.

BL Chalet Girl economy tip
Don't throw away pieces of cake that have gone stale. Use as the basis of a trifle.

ZUCCHINI BREAD

175 g (6 oz) margarine
225 g (8 oz) sugar
4 eggs
2 large courgettes (zucchini), grated
150 ml (¼ pint) water
500 g (1 lb 2 oz) plain flour, sifted
10 ml (2 teaspoons) bicarbonate of soda
2.5 ml (½ teaspoon) baking powder
5 ml (1 teaspoon) cinnamon
2.5 ml (½ teaspoon) ground cloves
5 ml (1 teaspoon) salt
175 g (6 oz) walnuts, chopped

(serves 10–14)

Mix the sugar and margarine together well. Add the eggs and courgettes (zucchini) and water. Then mix in all the dry ingredients. Pour into a greased 1 kilo (2 lb) loaf tin and bake in a pre-heated moderate oven (350°F, 180°C, gas 4) for 1–1¼ hours.

Chalet girl comment: I got the recipe from an American friend – it is unusual and easy to do.

FRUITY SCONES

225 g (8 oz) self-raising flour
25 g (1 oz) butter or firm margarine
50 g (2 oz) granulated sugar
pinch of salt
150 ml (¼ pint) milk
225 g (8 oz) raisins or sultanas

(serves 6–8)

Put the flour and sugar in a large mixing bowl and rub in the fat. Mix in the dried fruit and salt, and then mix in the milk with a knife to make a soft dough. Pat this mixture onto a floured board, until it is about 4 cm (1½ in) thick. Cut into rounds or squares and bake for 6–7 minutes in a hot oven (450°F, 230°C, gas 8).

During a rather snowy week when skiing was impossible, a party of bored young farmers decided to amuse themselves by setting traps for each other round the chalet. They dug holes and disguised them with flimsy coverings that were soon camouflaged by the snow. While some of them were round the back digging another, the delivery man arrived round the front and promptly disappeared. The chalet girl found him as he struggled out, far from amused. Not even bribery would convince him to deliver to that chalet again.

DALY'S DROP SCONES

225 g (8 oz) plain flour
50 g (2 oz) sugar
2.5 ml (½ teaspoon) bicarbonate of soda

5 ml (1 teaspoon) cream of tartar
2 eggs
300 ml (½ pint) milk
lard or oil for frying

(serves 6)

Sieve dry ingredients into a bowl. Make a well in the centre and add the eggs. Stirring from the centre, gradually add the milk, until all the flour is incorporated. Beat for a few minutes, and then leave to rest for 10 minutes. Brush a thick frying pan or griddle with lard or oil. When hot, drop spoonfuls of the mixture onto the pan. Cook for three minutes on each side. Wrap in a cloth to keep warm and soft while you make the rest. If necessary, re-grease before each batch.

Chalet girl comment: These are delicious hot with butter and jam, but they are also good cold.

CHOC MUNCHIES

225 g (8 oz) broken digestive biscuits
125 g (4 oz) margarine or butter
45 ml (3 tablespoons) syrup

125 g (4 oz) granulated sugar
50 g (2 oz) raisins
15 ml (1 tablespoon) cocoa
1 beaten egg

(serves 6)

Crush the biscuits with a rolling pin – but don't make the pieces too small. Melt the fat, sugar and syrup together in a pan with the raisins. Add the cocoa. Remove from the heat and add the beaten egg quickly. Stir in the broken biscuits. Put into a flat, greased biscuit tin or dish, and press down firmly. The mixture should be about 2.5 cm (1 in) thick. Leave to set and cool in the fridge. Turn out and cut into squares.

Chalet girl comment: These are very filling and more-ish. If you want to make them even more yummy you can melt 225 g (8 oz) plain chocolate and spread it on the top.

> *BL Chalet Girl kitchen planner tip*
> If you have no bread bin, use a good bag to hang it up in, as it helps stop crumbs going everywhere and keeps it fresh.

COCOA SHORTBREAD THUMBS

125 g (4 oz) self-raising flour, sifted
50 g (2 oz) granulated sugar
75 g (3 oz) margarine

icing
125 g (4 oz) icing sugar, sifted
15 ml (1 tablespoon) cocoa powder, sifted

25 g (1 oz) lard
25 g (1 oz) cornflour
25 g (1 oz) cocoa

25 g (1 oz) butter
50 g (2 oz) glacé cherries

(serves 6)

Mix and knead all the ingredients together. Roll into balls and put on a greased tray about 5 cm (2 in) apart, and press a dent in each one with your thumb. Bake in a moderate oven (300°F, 150°C, gas 3) for 20–25 minutes. When cool, put a teaspoon of icing (made with the icing sugar, cocoa powder and softened butter beaten together and mixed with a little water) in each dent, and put a cherry on the top.

DRINKS

In standard chalets Bladon Lines customers can drink as much wine as they like with their dinner, but most of them love punch or cocktails too. The heavy drinkers (notably farmers, doctors and the army!) like them powerful, but some of the customers prefer brews that are benign and alcohol-free. This is a small selection of the favourites.

THE TEN DAYS OF SKI SCHOOL

A Glühwein Song

(to the tune of 'The Twelve Days of Christmas')

On the first day of ski school my instructor said to me:
'Put your weight on your downhill ski'
On the second day . . . (etc.)
'Bend both your knees'
Third . . .
'Don't lean back'
Fourth . . .
'Swing both your hips'
Fifth . . .
'Ski parallel'
Sixth . . .
'Face down the mountain'
Seventh . . .
'Turn on the moguls'
Eighth . . .
'Wedel down the short bits'
Ninth . . .
'Schluss down the straight bits'
Tenth . . .
'Let's try a ski jump'

BANANA EGG FLIP

2 bananas
600 ml (1 pint) milk
1 egg
30 ml (2 tablespoons) sugar

(serves 2/3)

Put all the ingredients in the blender and mix on maximum speed for 2–3 minutes.

TIGGER'S BELLINI

bottle champagne (or sparkling wine).
4 peaches

(8 glasses)

Blanch and peel the peaches. Purée them in a blender and mix with the champagne.

HARRY'S LIME

lime juice (fresh or Rose's cordial)
lemonade
ice cream

Fill long glasses with crushed ice. Add a little lime juice to each glass and top up with lemonade. Float a scoop of creamy ice cream on the top. Decorate each glass with a twist of fresh lime or lemon.

Chalet girl comment: For confirmed tipplers, add a dash of dacquiri, vodka, or both!

POTENT PUNCH

bottle of cheap red wine
bottle of strong cider
large carton of orange juice or apple juice
10 cm (4 in) cinnamon stick

10 cloves
brown sugar to taste
oranges and/or apples, peeled and chopped

(16 glasses)

Mix the red wine and fruit juice with the cinnamon stick and cloves, and leave overnight. Before serving, heat the wine mixture with sugar to taste until the sugar has dissolved. Do not boil. Add the fruit and allow to get very hot. Ladle into a serving jug and top up with the cider.

Chalet girl comment: Warning! This is a lethal drug! Do not exceed the stated dose of 2 glasses or you will not be responsible for your actions! To make the punch even more potent, add a drop of cheap brandy to the warmed mixture.

THE DIETER'S FRIEND

125 g (4 oz) strawberries
large carton orange juice

600 ml (1 pint) Perrier or soda water

(8 long glasses)

Purée the strawberries in a blender. Mix the strawberries with the orange juice. Fill long glasses half-full with crushed ice and pour the strawberry mixture over it. Top up with the Perrier water or soda water. Decorate each glass with a strawberry and half a slice of orange.

Chalet girl comment: You can drink to your heart's content and gaze with delight at your slim figure in the mirror!

TAQUINERIE'S SPECIAL VIN CHAUD

bottle red wine
left-over, duty-free drink (gin, whisky, vodka, rum, etc.)

sugar to taste
2 vin chaud spice bags
10 cm (4 in) cinnamon stick

(serves 2–4)

Empty the bottle of red wine into a saucepan. Add as many measures of your chosen spirit as you want (or have left). Put in the cinnamon stick, spice bags and sugar to taste. Heat gently until quite hot, but do not boil.

THE PICKLED PARROT

15 ml (1 tablespoon) caster sugar
90 ml (6 tablespoons) brandy
90 ml (6 tablespoons) orange curaçao
45 ml (3 tablespoons) maraschino

45 ml (3 tablespoons) grand marnier
1.2 litres (2 pints) sparkling wine

(10 glasses)

Put ingredients into a large bowl. Add ice, stir well, and decorate with orange and pineapple slices.

Chalet girl comment: A very welcoming drink. It tastes incredible and helps the cooking – and the washing-up!

Index

almonds: amandines potatoes, 94
   biscuit Tortini, 123
   broccoli bouton d'or, 97
   cauliflower with almonds, 101
   deep-fried Camembert, 40
   gâteau montagne, 113
   tarte aux abricots, 118
amandines potatoes, 94
apples: apple and grape salad with mint dressing, 104
   apple sauce, 74
   apple scones, 139
   cider-baked pork chops, 79
   gâteau montagne, 113
   hazelnut galette, 124
   potato, onion and apple Dauphinoise, 94-5
   poulet à la Vallée d'Auge, 65
   poulet normande, 66
   stuffed grapefruit, 27
   Swiss apple tart, 122
   thirteen star salad, 26
   yoghurt apple brûlée, 129
   Zermatt apple tarts, 120
apricots: apricot ambrosia, 132
   apricot crumble party slice, 141
   apricot sauce, 40
   Taquinerie cheesecake, 112
   tarte aux abricots, 118
asparagus, veal with, 55
aubergines: moussakka, 52
   stuffed aubergines, 42
Austrian Linzertorte, 143
avocado: avocado les Allues, 43
   avocado Marseilles, 32
   avocado pâté aux quatre saisons, 26-7
   baked avocado, 34
   Cary's Courmayeur cocotte, 18
   creamed chicken and avocado, 66

bacon: avocado les Allues, 43
   bacon cream, 19
   Cary's Courmayeur cocotte, 18
   courgette canoes with bacon and tomato, 44-5
   Crans Montana ramekins, 20
   Gstaad mushrooms, 34
   poulet de Dijon, 69
   poulet normande, 66
   Wintersonne soup, 23
baked avocado, 34
bananas: banana bread, 139
   banana egg flip, 151
   banana ice cream, 124
   banana pudding à la Charlet, 115
   Banoffi pie, 108
   chocolate willies, 131
   citrus surprise, 130-1
   crème Clarmont, 135
   monkey's delight, 29
   toffee treat, 119
Banoffi pie, 108
basil, sauté potatoes with, 92
béchamel sauce, 77
beef: cheesy beef rolls, 53
   chili con carne, 52-3
   fillet of beef en croûte, 50
   Kitzbuhel creamed beef, 50
   mousakka, 52
   spinach and Ricotta gratin, 49
beetroot: Mazot salad, 102
biscuit Tortini, 123
biscuits: cocoa shortbread thumbs, 147
Bladon Lines gougère, 77
blue cheese: Cary's Courmayeur cocotte, 18
   Gorgonzola mousse, 28
   loin of pork with blue cheese, 81
   pear vinaigrette, 40
   poire Roquefort, 22
   thirteen star salad, 26
   see also cheese; cream and soft cheese
Boursin cheese, Clarmont turkey, 60
brandy: biscuit Tortini, 123
   brandy and ginger cream, 134
   meringue Meribel, 116
   the pickled parrot, 153
bread: croûtons, 46

garlic bread, 46
herb bread, 45
pansanella, 44
broccoli: broccoli bouton d'or, 97
   chicken Chicheley, 62

cabbage: cabbage with nutmeg, 100
   lemon cabbage, 101
   see also red cabbage
cakes, 137-47
   apricot crumble party slice, 141
   Austrian Linzertorte, 143
   banana bread, 139
   choc munchies, 146
   chocolate ripple cake, 140
   energy cake, 141
   orange syrup cake, 142
   strawberry cake, 142
   yoghurt cake, 140
Camembert cheese: Camembert surprise, 38
   deep-fried Camembert, 40
caramel: Banoffi pie, 108
   oranges in caramel, 134-5
   toffee treat, 119
carrots: carrots in white sauce, 97
   glazed carrots, 98
   kipper and vegetable bake, 86
   lemon-glazed carrots, 97
   mashed potato and carrot, 96
   salad al dente, 103
   le Trois Vallées trio, 100
Cary's Courmayeur cocotte, 18
cauliflower: cauliflower with almonds, 101
   salad al dente, 103
celery: chicken and celery Chancard, 64-5
   le Trois Vallées trio, 100
Chamonix cheesecake, 107
champagne: Tigger's Bellini, 151
champignons à la crème, 35
charlotte aux framboises et fromage blanc, 136
cheese: bacon cream, 19
   baked avocado, 34
   cheesy beef rolls, 53
   chicken and celery Chancard, 64-5
   chicken Chicheley, 62
   cider-baked pork chops, 79
   courgette canoes with bacon and tomato, 44-5
   Crans Montana ramekins, 20
   croissants à la maison rose, 30
   deep-fried mushrooms with herb cheese, 32
   Delmonica potatoes, 92
   devilled mushrooms, 35
   Flemish eggs, 22
   haddock surprise, 23
   lamb cutlet le Cairn, 72
   leeks in cheese sauce, 98
   Lucrezia special, 64
   Luigi's pizza, 86-7
   monkey's delight, 29
   oeuf en cocotte, 21
   pork Parmesan with tomato sauce, 76
   salmon ramekins, 18-19
   seafood crumble, 84
   spinach ramekin, 20
   stuffed aubergines, 42
   vegetarian lasagne, 88
   see also blue cheese; cream and soft cheese
cheesecakes: Chamonix cheesecake, 107
   frozen chocolate cheesecake, 110
   Matterhorn cheesecake, 111
   Nioby flan, 112
   no-cheese cheesecake, 110
   Taquinerie cheesecake, 112
cherries: brandy and ginger cream, 134
cherry brandy: snow-capped mountains, 131
chicken: chicken and celery Chancard, 64-5
   chicken and pineapple casserole, 57
   chicken Chicheley, 62
   chicken Provençal, 56
   coronation chicken, 60
   creamed chicken and avocado, 66
   French-fried chicken, 62
   lemon chicken Courmayeur, 71
   lemon honey chicken, 57
   Lucrezia special, 64
   mango chicken, 63
   poulet à la Vaillée d'Auge, 65
   poulet de Dijon, 69
   poulet normande, 66
   spiced chicken, 59
chicory: thirteen star salad, 26
chili con carne, 52-3

chocolate: choc munchies, 146
  choccy biccy pud, 128
  chocolate honey
    profiteroles, 119
  chocolate ripple cake, 140
  chocolate roulade, 123
  chocolate willies, 131
  cocoa shortbread thumbs, 147
  dark and white chocolate
    parfait, 126
  energy cake, 141
  frozen chocolate
    cheesecake, 110
  Klosters chocolate krunch, 136
  Norwegian cream, 132
  nostalgia pudding, 120
  rich chocolate gâteau, 129
  snow-capped mountains, 131
choux pastry: amandines
    potatoes, 94
  Bladon Lines gougère, 77
  chocolate honey
    profiteroles, 119
cider: cider-baked pork chops, 79
  pork and orange chops, 78-9
  potent punch, 152
  poulet normande, 66
citrus surprise, 130-1
Clarmont turkey, 60
cocoa shortbread thumbs, 147
cod: Jo's cod parcels, 84
coffee and Kahlua syllabub, 126
condensed milk: Banoffi pie, 108
  toffee treat, 119
consommé, eggs in, 18
cornflakes: Klosters chocolate
    krunch, 136
  le Perroquet lemon freeze, 108
coronation chicken, 60
Courchevel courgettes, 102
Courcheval quail, 61
courgettes: Courchevel
    courgettes, 102
  courgette canoes with bacon and
    tomato, 44-5
  salad al dente, 103
  zucchini bread, 144
Crans Montana ramekins, 20
cream: champignons à la crème, 35
  chocolate ripple cake, 140
  crème Clarmont, 135
  Delmonica potatoes, 92
  meringue Meribel, 116
  le Perroquet lemon freeze, 108

cream, soured see soured cream
cream and soft cheese: Camembert
    surprise, 38
  Chamonix cheesecake, 107
  charlotte aux framboises et
    fromage blanc, 136
  Clarmont turkey, 60
  crème Clarmont, 135
  deep-fried Camembert, 40
  frozen chocolate
    cheesecake, 110
  lemon biscuit pudding, 109
  Matterhorn cheesecake, 111
  moussaka, 52
  Nioby flan, 112
  pork Stroganoff, 78
  prawns and spinach en
    cocotte, 16
  spinach and Ricotta gratin, 49
  stuffed grapefruit, 27
  Taquinerie cheesecake, 112
  tuna mousse, 15
  see also blue cheese; cheese
creamed chicken and
    avocado, 66
crème Clarmont, 135
crème patissière, 118, 122
crêpes, seafood, 85
croissants à la maison rose, 30
croûtons, 46
crumble, seafood, 84
crunchy-topped pork chops, 73
cucumber: Mazot salad, 102
  pansanella, 44
  spiced chicken, 59
Cumberland sauce, 72
curry: coronation chicken, 60

dark and white chocolate
    parfait, 126
deep-fried Camembert, 40
deep-fried mushrooms with
    garlic mayonnaise, 39
deep-fried mushrooms with herb
    cheese, 32
Delmonica potatoes, 92
devilled mushrooms, 35
The dieter's friend, 152
Dijon roast pork, 74
double-quick pâté, 15
dressings: mint, 104
  sweet vinaigrette, 104
  vinaigrette, 104
drinks, 149-53

drop scones, Daly's, 146

eggs: banana egg flip, 151
　　Crans Montana ramekins, 20
　　eggs in consommé, 18
　　Flemish eggs, 22
　　oeuf en cocotte, 21
　　salami en cocotte, 16
　　salmon ramekins, 18-19
energy cake, 141

fillet of beef en croûte, 50
fish: seafood crêpes, 85
　　seafood crumble, 84
　　seafood envelopes, 36-7
　　soupe de poisson, 24-5
　　see also individual types of fish
Flemish eggs, 22
French-fried chicken, 62
frogs' legs: grenouilles, 24
frozen chocolate cheesecake, 110
fruit: fruit salad St Moritz, 125
　　yoghurt pudding, 128
　　see also individual types of fruit
fruity scones, 144

galette, hazelnut, 124
garlic: deep-fried mushrooms with garlic mayonnaise, 39
　　garlic bread, 46
gâteaux: gâteau montagne, 113
　　rich chocolate gâteau, 129
ginger biscuits: brandy and ginger cream, 134
glazed carrots, 98
Gorgonzola mousse, 28
gougère, Bladon Lines, 77
Granny's pork chops, 78
grapefruit, stuffed, 27
grapes: apple and grape salad with mint dressing, 104
gratin, spinach and Ricotta, 49
grenouilles, 24
Gstaad mushrooms, 34

haddock surprise, 23
ham: Bladon Lines gougère, 77
　　croissants à la maison rose, 30
　　haddock surprise, 23
　　monkey's delight, 29
　　stuffed aubergines, 42
Harry's lime, 151
hazelnuts: hazelnut galette, 124
　　turkey and hazelnuts, 70

herb bread, 45
honey: chocolate honey profiteroles, 119
　　glazed carrots, 98
　　Granny's pork chops, 78
　　lemon honey chicken, 57
　　pork à l'orange, 80

ice cream: banana ice cream, 124
　　biscuit Tortini, 123
　　dark and white chocolate parfait, 126
　　Harry's lime, 151
　　Mars bar sauce for vanilla ice cream, 128-9
　　meringue ice cream, 117
　　very easy lemon ice cream, 134

Jo's cod parcels, 84
Kahlua and coffee syllabub, 126
kipper and vegetable bake, 86
Kitzbuhel creamed beef, 50
Klosters chocolate krunch, 136

lamb: lamb boulangère, 71
　　lamb cutlet le Cairn, 72
　　lasagne, vegetarian, 88
leeks: leek and potato bake, 96
　　leeks in cheese sauce, 98
lemon: banana ice cream, 124
　　lemon biscuit pudding, 109
　　lemon cabbage, 101
　　lemon can't-leave-me-alone pudding, 130
　　lemon chicken Courmayeur, 71
　　lemon-glazed carrots, 97
　　lemon honey chicken, 57
　　no-cheese cheesecake, 110
　　le Perroquet lemon freeze, 108
　　Tignes turkey tit-bits, 68
　　very easy lemon ice cream, 134
lemonade: Harry's lime, 151
lettuce: pasta à l'indienne, 30
lime: Harry's lime, 151
　　melon in lime, 130
Linzertorte, Austrian, 143
loin of pork with blue cheese, 81
Lucrezia special, 64
Luigi's pizza, 86-7

mackerel: smoked mackerel pâté, 13
main courses, 47-88
mangetout: le Trois Vallées

158

trio, 100
mango chicken, 63
marinated mushrooms, 26
marmalade: nostalgia pudding, 120
Mars bar sauce for vanilla ice cream, 128-9
marsala: biscuit Tortini, 123
mashed potato and carrot, 96
Matterhorn cheesecake, 111
mayonnaise: avocado Marseilles, 32
   chicken Chicheley, 62
   coronation chicken, 60
   deep-fried mushrooms with garlic mayonnaise, 39
   pasta à l'indienne, 30
   salad al dente, 103
Mazot salad, 102
melon in lime, 130
meringue: banana pudding à la Charlet, 115
   gâteau montagne, 113
   meringue ice cream, 117
   meringue Meribel, 116
   strawberry Pavlova, 116
Mexican red pepper soup, 43
milk: banana egg flip, 151
mint: apple and grape salad with mint dressing, 104
monkey's delight, 29
moussaka, 52
mousses: Gorgonzola mousse, 28
   tuna mousse, 15
muesli: energy cake, 141
mushrooms: baked avocado, 34
   Bladon Lines gougère, 77
   champignons à la crème, 35
   chicken and pineapple casserole, 57
   chicken Provençal, 56
   cider-baked pork chops, 79
   croissants à la maison rose, 30
   deep-fried mushrooms with garlic mayonnaise, 39
   deep-fried mushrooms with herb cheese, 32
   devilled mushrooms, 35
   fillet of beef en croûte, 50
   Gstaad mushrooms, 34
   Jo's cod parcels, 84
   kipper and vegetable bake, 86
   Lucrezia special, 64
   marinated mushrooms, 26
   mushroom Stroganoff, 36
   mushrooms à la Lamastra, 31
   pork and mushroom parcels, 82
   pork Stroganoff, 78
   poulet de Dijon, 69
   space suit porkies, 73
   turkey escalopes aux champignons, 68
   veal Val d'Isère, 54
   vegetarian lasagne, 88
mussels: seafood crumble, 84
   seafood envelopes, 36-7
   soupe de poisson, 24-5
mustard: Dijon roast pork, 74
   French-fried chicken, 62
   Granny's pork chops, 78
   poulet de Dijon, 69
   Zermatt potatoes, 91

Nioby flan, 112
no-cheese cheesecake, 110
noodles: Kitzbuhel creamed beef, 50
   noodles Haute Nendaz, 103
Norwegian cream, 132
nostalgia pudding, 120
nutmeg, cabbage with, 100
nuts: yoghurt pudding, 128

oeuf en cocotte, 21
olives: chicken Provençal, 56
onions: potato, onion and apple Dauphinoise, 94-5
   tarte à l'oignon, 38
orange: banana ice cream, 124
   chocolate roulade, 123
   Courchevel quail, 61
   the dieter's friend, 152
   Jo's cod parcels, 84
   Klosters chocolate krunch, 136
   orange syrup cake, 142
   oranges in caramel, 134-5
   pork à l'orange, 80
   pork and orange chops, 78-9
   pork chops Grindelwald, 80-1
   red cabbage and orange, 100-1
   thirteen star salad, 26

pansanella, 44
paprika potatoes, 91
Parmesan cheese: pork Parmesan with tomato sauce, 76
parsnip soup, 28
party baked potatoes, 92-3
pasta: Lucrezia special, 64
   pasta à l'indienne, 30

pastry, choux, 77
pâtés and terrines: avocado pâte aux
    quatre saisons, 26-7
  Courchevel quail, 61
  double-quick pâté, 15
  fillet of beef en croûte, 50
  St Anton sardine pâté, 14-15
  smoked mackerel pâté, 13
  tuna fish and spinach terrine, 14
Pavlova, strawberry, 116
peaches: Nioby flan, 112
  Tigger's Bellini, 151
Peanuts: crunch-topped pork
    chops, 73
  deep-fried Camembert, 40
  pasta à l'indienne, 30
pears: pear vinaigrette, 40
  poire Roquefort, 22
peppers: avocado Marseilles, 32
  chicken and pineapple
    casserole, 57
  Delmonica potatoes, 92
  Mexican red pepper soup, 43
  noodles Haute Nendaz, 103
  pansanella, 44
  spiced chicken, 59
  stuffed grapefruit, 27
  Wintersonne soup, 23
Le Perroquet lemon freeze, 108
The pickled parrot, 153
pies and pastries: Camembert
    surprise, 38
  fillet of beef en croûte, 50
  hazelnut galette, 124
  lamb cutlet le Cairn, 72
  pork and mushroom parcels, 82
  seafood envelopes, 36-7
  toffee treat, 119
pilaff, rice, 59
pimento: chicken and pineapple
    casserole, 57
pineapple, chicken and pineapple
    casserole, 57
  crème Clarmont, 135
  Matterhorn cheesecake, 111
pizza, Luigi's, 86-7
poire Roquefort, 22
pork: cider-baked pork chops, 79
  crunchy-topped pork chops, 73
  Dijon roast pork, 74
  Granny's pork chops, 78
  loin of pork with blue cheese, 81
  pork à l'orange, 80
  pork and mushroom parcels, 82

pork and orange chops, 78-9
pork chops Grindelwald, 80-1
pork Parmesan with tomato
    sauce, 76
pork Stroganoff, 78
space suit porkies, 73
posh baked potatoes, 93
potato: amandines potatoes, 94
  Delmonica potatoes, 92
  lamb boulangère, 71
  leek and potato bake, 96
  mashed potato and carrot, 96
  paprika potatoes, 91
  party baked potatoes, 92-3
  posh baked potatoes, 93
  potato, onion and apple
    Dauphinoise, 94-5
  sauté potatoes with basil, 92
  Zermatt potatoes, 91
potent punch, 152
poulet à la Vallée d'Auge, 65
poulet de Dijon, 69
poulet normande, 66
prawns: Crans Montana
    ramekins, 20
  haddock surprise, 23
  oeuf en cocotte, 21
  prawns and spinach en
    cocotte, 16
  seafood crêpes, 85
  seafood crumble, 84
  seafood envelopes, 36-7
  soupe de poisson, 24-5
profiteroles, chocolate honey, 119
puddings, 105-36
punch, potent, 152

quail, Courchevel, 61

raisins: fruity scones, 144
raspberries: banana pudding à la
    Charlet, 115
  brandy and ginger cream, 134
  charlotte aux framboises et
    fromage blanc, 136
  dark and white chocolate
    parfait, 126
  meringue ice cream, 117
  meringue Meribel, 116
red cabbage and orange, 100-1
  see also cabbage
red kidney beans: chili con
    carne, 52-3
redcurrants: Courchevel quail, 61

Cumberland sauce, 72
   melon in lime, 130
rice: rice salad, 103
   Spanish-method rice, 96
   spiced chicken, 59
rich chocolate gateau, 129
Ricotta cheese: spinach and Ricotta gratin, 49
Roquefort, poire, 22
roulade, chocolate, 123

St Anton sardine pâté, 14-15
salads and vegetables, 89-104
   apple and grape salad with mint dressing, 104
   cucumber salad, 59
   Mazot salad, 102
   noodles Haute Nendaz, 103
   rice salad, 103
   salad al dente, 103
   thirteen star salad, 26
salami: Luigi's pizza, 86-7
   salami en cocotte, 16
salmon ramekins, 18-19
sardines: St Anton sardine pâté, 14-15
sauces: apple, 74
   apricot, 40
   béchamel, 77
   cheese, 98
   Cumberland, 72
   Mars bar sauce for vanilla ice cream, 128-9
   raspberry, 126
   tomato, 54-5, 76
   see also dressings
sausages: pasta à l'indienne, 30
   see also salami
sauté potatoes with basil, 92
scones: apple scones, 139
   fruity scones, 144
seafood crêpes, 85
seafood crumble, 84
seafood envelopes, 36-7
shortbread thumbs, cocoa, 147
smoked haddock: haddock surprise, 23
smoked mackerel pâté, 13
snow-capped mountains, 131
soups: Mexican red pepper soup, 43
   parsnip soup, 28
   soupe de poisson, 24-5
   Wintersonne soup, 23
soured cream: cheesy beef rolls, 53

Kitzbuhel creamed beef, 50
   mushroom Stroganoff, 36
   spiced chicken, 59
space suit porkies, 73
Spanish-method rice, 96
spiced chicken, 59
spinach: prawns and spinach en cocotte, 16
   St Anton sardine pâté, 14-15
   spinach and Ricotta gratin, 49
   spinach ramekin, 20
   tuna fish and spinach terrine, 14
starters, 11-46
steamed puddings: nostalgia pudding, 120
Stilton cheese: Cary's Courmayeur cocotte, 18
   loin of pork with blue cheese, 81
   pear vinaigrette, 40
strawberries: banana pudding à la Charlet, 115
   the dieter's friend, 152
   meringue Meribel, 116
   strawberry cake, 142
   strawberry Pavlova, 116
stuffed aubergines, 42
stuffed grapefruit, 27
sultanas: fruity scones, 144
   pasta à l'indienne, 30
   thirteen star salad, 26
sweet vinaigrette, 104
sweetcorn: Bladon Lines gougère, 77
   Lucrezia special, 64
   noodles Haute Nendaz, 103
Swiss apple tart, 122
syllabub, coffee and Kahlua, 126

Taquinerie cheesecake, 112
Taquinerie's special vin chaud, 153
tarts: Banoffi pie, 108
   lemon biscuit pudding, 109
   Le Perroguet lemon freeze, 108
   Swiss apple tart, 122
   tarte à l'oignon, 38
   tarte aux abricots, 118
   Zermatt apple tarts, 120
   see also cheesecakes
teabreads: zucchini bread, 144
terrines *see* pâtés and terrines
thirteen star salad, 26
Tigger's Bellini, 151
Tignes turkey tit-bits, 68
toffee treat, 119

tomato: Bladon Lines gougère, 77
  Cary's Courmayeur cocotte, 18
  chicken Provençal, 56
  chili con carne, 52-3
  courgette canoes with bacon and tomato, 44-5
  Luigi's pizza, 86-7
  moussaka, 52
  pansanella, 44
  paprika potatoes, 91
  pork Parmesan with tomato sauce, 76
  soupe de poisson, 24-5
  stuffed aubergines, 42
  veal chignons in tomato sauce, 54-5
  vegetarian lasagne, 88
  Wintersonne soup, 23
Le Trois Vallées trio, 100
tuna: baked avocado, 34
  double-quick pâté, 15
  pansanella, 44
  tuna fish and spinach terrine, 14
  tuna fish creams, 13
  tuna mousse, 15
turkey: Clarmont turkey, 60
  Tignes turkey tit-bits, 68
  turkey and hazelnuts, 70
  turkey escalopes aux champignons, 68

veal: veal chignons in tomato sauce, 54-5
  veal Val d'Isère, 54
  veal with asparagus, 55
vegetables and salads, 89-104
vegetarian lasagne, 88
very easy lemon ice cream, 134
vinaigrette, 104
  pear vinaigrette, 40
  sweet, 104

walnuts: banana pudding à la Charlet, 115
  frozen chocolate cheesecake, 110
  Gstaad mushrooms, 34
  Jo's cod parcels, 84
  zucchini bread, 144
white sauce, carrots in, 97
wine: avocado pâté aux quatre saisons, 26-7
  cheesy beef rolls, 53
  chicken Provençal, 56
  chocolate ripple cake, 140

Clarmont turkey, 60
Gstaad mushrooms, 34
marinated mushrooms, 26
Mexican red pepper soup, 43
the pickled parrot, 153
potent punch, 152
Taquinerie's special vin chaud, 153
veal chignons in tomato sauce, 54-5
Wintersonne soup, 23

yoghurt: brandy and ginger cream, 134
  chicken and celery Chancard, 64-5
  citrus surprise, 130-1
  Mazot salad, 102
  thirteen star salad, 26
  yoghurt apple brûlée, 129
  yoghurt cake, 140
  yoghurt pudding, 128

Zermatt apple tarts, 120
Zermatt potatoes, 91
zucchini bread, 144